BLACK BOOK®

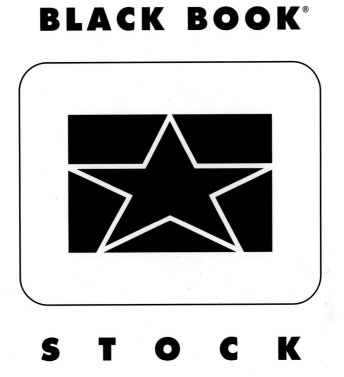

S T O C K

1992

"Black Book Stock" is a trademark of
Black Book Marketing Group,
a Division of Macmillan, Inc.

HEADQUARTERS:

Black Book Marketing Group
115 Fifth Ave.
New York, NY 10003
Telephone (212) 254-1330
Facsimile (212) 598-4497

ADVERTISING SALES OFFICES:

CHICAGO
212 W. Superior St., Ste. 203
Chicago, IL 60610
Telephone (312) 944-5115
Facsimile (312) 944-7865

LOS ANGELES
8981 Sunset Blvd., Ste. 309
Los Angeles, CA 90069
Telephone (310) 858-0013
Facsimile (310) 858-0083

CINCINNATI
117-121 E. Court St.
Cincinnati, OH 45202
Telephone (513) 632-5320
Facsimile (513) 721-5824

DALLAS
Plaza Suites at Centrum
3102 Oak Lawn, Ste. 700
Dallas, TX 75219
Telephone (214) 521-8066
Facsimile (214) 526-5660

MIAMI
3841 N.E. Second Ave., Ste. 202
Miami, FL 33137
Telephone (305) 573-6456
Facsimile (305) 576-2617

MINNEAPOLIS
401 N. Third St., Ste. 400,
Minneapolis, MN 55401
Telephone (612) 338-9044
Facsimile (612) 338-9050

SAN FRANCISCO
450 Alabama St.
San Francisco, CA 94110
Telephone (415) 431-8080
Facsimile (415) 554-0503

PRESIDENT ★ H. Huntington Stehli

PUBLISHER ★ John P. Frenville

Assistant to the Publisher: Karen Price

SALES DIRECTOR ★ Rob Drasin

Assistant to the Sales Director: Deborah Poole

Account Representatives: Sharon Ames, Roxanne Brown, Diane Casey, Francoise Dubois, Phyllis Giarnese, David Morrison, Katie Ross, Amy Wheeler

Administrative Staff: Kathy De Lorenzo, Margaret Kenny, Phyllipa Lyttle, Tosca Marcy, Tammy Schwartz, Katie Rehm

CREATIVE DIRECTOR ★ Lori H. McDaniel

Art Director: Paul Young

Assistant: Mimi Weisel

PRODUCTION DIRECTOR ★ Meggin Chinkel

Project Coordinator: Jason Taback

Coordinator: Christina Holbrook

Traffic: John Siemens

DISTRIBUTION/LISTING DIRECTOR ★ Lucille Friedman

Assistant Distribution/Listings Manager: Me'Shel Riedel

Staff: Brian Celiberti, Kent McDaniel, Robert Sefcik, Cynthia Thomas

PROMOTION DIRECTOR ★ Mitchell Engelmeyer

Art Director: Janet Giampietro

BUSINESS MANAGER ★ Christopher E. Lenzi

Controller: Irving Wiener

Staff: Cynthia Riley, Michael Rispoli, Steve Schmidt, Gayle Walker

Black Book Stock is distributed in the U.S. and Canada by:
Black Book Marketing Group
115 Fifth Ave., New York, NY 10003
Telephone (212) 254-1330, Facsimile (212) 598-4497

Black Book Stock is distributed outside of the U.S. and Canada by:
Hearst Books International
1350 Ave. of the Americas, New York, NY 10019
Telephone (212) 261-6770, Facsimile (212) 261-6795

ISBN 0-916098-69-9 / ISSN 0738-9000

Printed in Hong Kong by Everbest Printing Co., Ltd
Color Separations by Rainbow Graphics Arts Co., Ltd

STAFF

In order to support the efforts of The Picture Agency Council of America (PACA), agency/client creative buyers and professional photographers, and to promote and maintain the highest standards of honesty, fairplay and productive relationships within the stock photography industry, Black Book Stock includes the PACA Code of Ethics.

CODE OF ETHICS

PICTURE AGENCY COUNCIL
OF AMERICA

Picture Agency Council of America Members will at all times endeavor to promote policies and practices that serve to elevate the stock photography industry, rigorously maintaining the highest standards of honesty and fair play with clients, photographers and each other.

Picture Agency Council of America Members commit themselves to the highest standard of services and products.

Picture Agency Council of America Members will comply with all applicable laws, rules and regulations.

Picture Agency Council of America Members will provide each employee of their respective agencies with a copy of this Code of Ethics and will encourage distribution of same to their photographers.

In addition, Picture Agency Council of America Members commit themselves to the following standards in the following areas:

STOCK AGENCY WITH PHOTOGRAPHER:

PACA Members will:

1. Be ethical in dealing with photographers.

2. Give all photographers equal treatment in representing their work.

3. Be mindful of the trust placed in them by photographers and always endeavor to promote the interest of the photographers they represent in tandem with their own.

4. Be willing to discuss the following items openly and honestly with their photographers:

   ★ Ownership of agency and/or change thereof.

   ★ Assignment policies, if applicable.

   ★ Editing, inventory and refilling procedures.

   ★ Disposition of any suit or settlement pertaining to a specific photographer's work, including documentation if requested.

   ★ Policies concerning photographer guarantees, if applicable.

   ★ Policies regarding free or reduced rate usages for charitable organizations.

   ★ International representation policies.

   ★ Sub-agency and franchise representation and policies.

5. Offer photographers a fair and straightforward written contract. Contract should address such items as:

   ★ Payment schedule.

   ★ Right to inspect agency records as they pertain to the individual photographer involved.

   ★ Procedure for handling lost and damaged photographs.

   ★ Contract period and renewal.

   ★ Charges, deductions or assessments related to the photographer's account.

   ★ Procedure and schedule for return of photographs upon termination of contract.

6. Scrupulously fulfill their contracts with photographers.

7. Provide photographers with payment in accordance with the Photographer/Agency contract. Statements should be sufficient for the photographer to correlate the end usage with the photograph in all domestic sales and every effort should be made to do the same in foreign sales. Statements should include:

   ★ An adequate photo description, as agreed upon between photographer and agency.

   ★ A description or code for the usage.

   ★ The amount of the photographer's share.

   ★ An itemization of any deductions that are made.

8. Take all reasonable steps to ensure copyright protection.

9. Use every reasonable effort to protect the physical safety of photographs.

10. Make every reasonable effort to secure proper photo credits where possible and appropriate, according to the terms of the delivery memos in use.

11. Make reasonable efforts to secure samples for photographers' portfolios.

12. Refrain from deceptive advertising.

13. Maintain confidentiality of records and information pertaining to individual photographers, except as required by law, or by terms of the Bylaws of Picture Agency Council of America.

STOCK AGENCY WITH CLIENT:

PACA members will:

1. Keep adequate sales records, when other than non-exclusive rights are being licensed, in an attempt to prevent possible conflicts in usage rights granted.

2. Make every effort to retrieve submitted photographs and to receive compensation for unreturned or damaged photographs.

3. Scrupulously avoid bribery of client, agency or employees.

4. Refrain from deceptive advertising.

5. Scrupulously honor all client confidentiality requests.

6. Be vigilant in protecting photographers' copyrights.

AGENCY WITH AGENCY:

PACA members will:

1. Actively promote originality of photographs in the interest of upholding the letter and the spirit of the copyright law and educate the photographic community concerning derivative uses of work.

2. Endeavor to respect the integrity of existing agency relationships with photographers and employees.

3. Refrain from soliciting information from new employees or photographers about their prior relationships with other agencies.

4. Aid in a smooth transition when photographers change agencies, in accordance with the contract. This includes retrieval and return of photographs, referrals to the new agency, and the communication of previous rights and information as necessary to prevent conflict.

5. Promptly return all material to a client who has inadvertently shipped returns to the wrong agency, after immediately notifying the client and the other photo agency that the materials are in the possession of the wrong agency.

JUST WHAT IS A STOCK PHOTO AGENCY?

If you need a photograph, there are two ways you can obtain it. You can hire a photographer to shoot it to your specifications or you can purchase the "use" of a photograph that already exists; that is, you can purchase a "stock" photograph. A stock photo agency is just what the name implies, an emporium where the product is existing photography.

HOW DOES ONE MAKE USE OF A STOCK AGENCY?

To make the most effective use of a stock agency, make contact with them at the inception of a project. The photo researcher who takes your call is a pro and has thorough knowledge of his or her file and may be able to offer constructive suggestions. The more information you supply about all aspects of your project, the better job they can and will do for you.

WHAT ABOUT THE COSTS?

Stock photography prices are determined not by the cost to produce the photograph or by the photographer's rate, but by the use of the photograph. The photograph used in a national ad campaign may be relatively expensive. The same photograph used in a small run magazine would cost only a fraction of that.

Since there is an almost infinite number of variables, it is impossible to actually list prices. The agency must strike a balance between making money for their photographers (and thereby ensure their source of supply) and realistically assessing the scope of a given project and pricing the photographs appropriately.

CARE OF TRANSPARENCIES

Transparencies are delicate and very valuable. Therefore, whether you get transparencies from an individual photographer or from a stock agency, you are responsible for returning all the transparencies safe and sound. That is why it is important that whoever handles the transparencies, whether it is an assistant, separator, or printer, be warned to avoid loss or damage of any kind.

PACA

CONTENTS

SUBJECT/CATEGORY INDEX

★ ★ ★ ★

★ ★ ★ ★ ★

★ ★ ★ ★ ★

★ ★ ★ ★ ★

★ ★ ★ ★ ★

SUBJECT	PAGE	SUBJECT	PAGE

★ ★ ★ ★

★ ★ ★ ★

★ ★ ★ ★

★ ★ ★ ★

★ ★ ★ ★

★ ★ ★ ★ ★

SUBJECT	PAGE	SUBJECT	PAGE

★ ★ ★ ★

IF
YOU CAN'T
SEE

EYE to EYE

SEE
US.

We're the Joint Ethics Committee–the people to see when business problems have you and your client at odds.

Since 1945, the JEC has been meeting monthly to act upon complaints and violations of its Code of Fair Practice. We arbitrate solutions to business disputes and ethical questions before they reach the often exasperating realm of the courts.

And we do it very inexpensively. Our arbitrators are concerned, objective volunteers from the advertising and graphic communication arts industries. They believe fair business dealings should be a right, not a fight.

If it sounds like you need our help, please write to us at P.O.Box 179, Grand Central Station, New York, NY 10163. Describe the problem you're having. Let's see what we can do.

To start a JEC chapter in your state: Request our brochure, "How to Establish a Joint Ethics Committee". For a copy of the Code of Fair Practice, please send five dollars.

JOINT ETHICS COMMITTEE

Arcaid

Architecture and interior design
photo library and
assignment photography
Telephone: 011 44 81 546 4352
Facsimile: 011 44 81 541 5230

1

DUOMO

DUOMO . . . the one source for sports photography . . . DUOMO . . .

the international stock and

assignment agency . . . DUOMO . . . worldwide coverage of sporting events and personalities

DUOMO . . . complete library of dynamic sports images . . . DUOMO

. . . the Olympic champions, the pros, and everyday athletes . . .

DUOMO . . . the challenge, the spirit, the ultimate victory . . .

. . . DUOMO . . . Official Games Photographers of the United

States Olympic Committee . . . DUOMO . . . the one source for sports photography . . . DUOMO

133 West 19th Street New York, NY 10011

OFFICIAL

GAMES PHOTOGRAPHERS

OF THE UNITED STATES

OLYMPIC COMMITTEE

telephone 212.243.1150 fax 212.633.1279

3

Historical Pictures Service, Inc.

921 W. VAN BUREN, SUITE 201
CHICAGO, ILLINOIS 60607
(312) 733-3239

FAX: (312) 733-2844

Benjamin Franklin

Johannes Gutenberg

Battle of Shiloh

Florence Nightingale

Franklin D. Roosevelt

Picnic (1883)

What If
All Dreams Came True?

What If The World
Wasn't Round?

What If Vacations
Lasted Forever?

What If Dogs
Could Talk?

What If SuperStock
Didn't Have It?

SUPERSTOCK
FOUR BY FIVE
800-828-4545

Call or write for free catalogs.

New York: Tel (212) 633-0300 Fax (212) 633-0408   San Francisco: Tel (415) 781-4433 Fax (415) 781-8985

Sales representatives are located in 54 offices around the world. See the Affiliates Index for complete listing.

Sipa Image

New York
30 West 21st Street, New York, N.Y.
10010 USA 212 463-0150
Tlx: 910240 8691
Fax: 212 463-0160

Paris
101 Boulevard Murat, 75016 Paris
Telephone: 47 43 47 43
Fax: 47 43 47 44

KIDS IN THE BIZ

... JUST A LITTLE BIT LICENSING HUMOUR ...

verkerke
mondadori group

LEO DE WYS

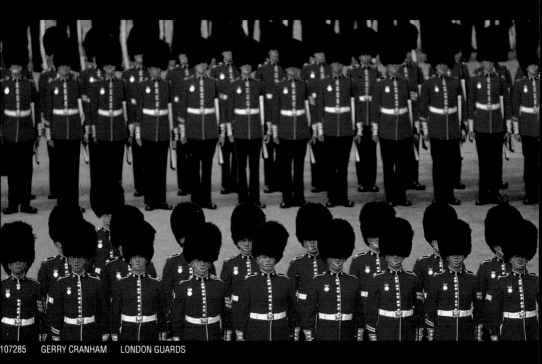

106544   BOB KRIST   NEW ORLEANS JAZZ

Leo de Wys INC

TEL 212-689-5580   FAX 212-545-1185   1-800-284-3399

106210   BEN BLANKENBURG

104207   CHRIS HUXLEY

48999   RICK RUSING

104297   RICK RUSING

107250   BOB KRIST   CARIBBEAN

82296   RICK RUSING

Leo de Wys INC

110247   JEAN PAUL NACIVET

109822   BILL BACHMAN

TEL 212-689-5580   FAX 212-545-1185   1-800-284-3399

19

ADVERTISING AUTOMOBILES

Performance and classic
cars. Studio or location. All
formats. If we don't have it,
we can get it.

If we don't have it, we can shoot it! Studio or location.

21

1960 Colony St., Mountain View, CA 94043 • 415/969-0682 • FAX 415/969-0485

KIMBALL STOCK

ADVERTISING ANIMALS

Galloping, growling, leaping, on wing, wild, domestic, exotic, dangerous. If we don't have it we can shoot it. Studio and location shots.

If we don't have it, we can shoot it! Studio or location.

KIMBALL STOCK

CULVER PICTURES, INC.

HISTORICAL STOCK IMAGES

150 West 22nd Street, Suite 300, New York, NY 10011

TEL (212) 645-1672   FAX (212) 627-9112

**THE MOST COMPLETE COLLECTION OF
MODERN MILITARY AIRCRAFT FROM AROUND THE WORLD.
WE OFFER SAME-DAY SERVICE OF ORIGINAL IMAGES VIA FEDERAL EXPRESS.
WRITE ON YOUR LETTERHEAD FOR THE "AIR POWER" DATE BOOK
AND CATALOG OF IMAGES.**

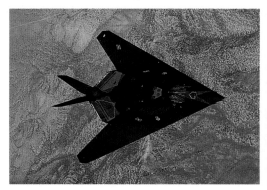

GEORGE HALL/CHECK SIX

426 Greenwood Beach

Tiburon, CA 94920

TEL 415.381.6363 / FAX 415.383.4935

**THE MOST COMPLETE COLLECTION OF
MODERN COMMERCIAL AIRLINERS AND CORPORATE AIRCRAFT.
WE OFFER SAME-DAY SERVICE OF ORIGINAL IMAGES VIA FEDERAL EXPRESS.
WRITE ON YOUR LETTERHEAD FOR THE "AIR POWER" DATE BOOK
AND CATALOG OF IMAGES.**

GEORGE HALL/CHECK SIX

426 Greenwood Beach

Tiburon, CA 94920

TEL 415.381.6363 / FAX 415.383.4935

© Lanny Johnson

MOUNTAIN STOCK

PHOTOGRAPHY & FILM, INC.

P.O. Box 1910, Tahoe City, California USA 96145

TEL 916•583•6646 / FAX 916•583•5935

© Nagel

© Kyle Krause

© Daryl Hunter

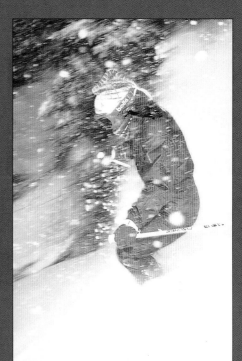
© John Clausen

© Chaco Mohler

© Bud Fawcett

© Garry Moore

© Simone

© Hank de Vre

© Bob Woodward

MOUNTAIN STOCK

PHOTOGRAPHY & FILM, INC.

P.O. Box 1910, Tahoe City, California USA 96145

TEL 916•583•6646 / FAX 916•583•5935

Kent Knudson

Scott Berner

The STOCKHOUSE Inc.

■

9261 Kirby Drive
Houston, Texas 77054
TEL 713-796-8400
FAX 713-796-8047

■

Bill Bachmann

Tom Campbell

PICTURE SYNDICATION

PICTURE SALES

PICTURE SALES

PHOTO & TEXT SYNDICATION

Henry Groskinsky

Robert Nickelsberg

Diana Walker

Ted Thai

Rudi Frey

Chris Niedenthal

TIME

PICTURE SYNDICATION

Time & Life Building, Rockefeller Center, New York, NY 10020, Fax: 212.522.0150

RENÉE MANCINI, MANAGER   212.522.3593

MARK SOLOMON, RESEARCH/SALES   212.522.3352

ABIGAIL SILZER, RESEARCH/SALES   212.522.3866

George Silk

LIFE

LIFE PICTURE SALES

Time & Life Building, Rockefeller Center, New York, NY 10020

TEL 212.522.4800 / FAX 212.522.0328

Andreas Feininger

Alfred Eisenstaedt

Dmitri Kessel

Alfred Eisenstaedt

35

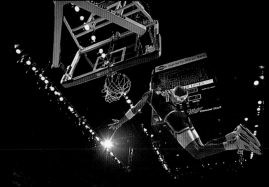

Walter Iooss Jr.

Sports Illustrated

PICTURE SALES
(212) 522-4781   (212) 522-0102 fax

Andy Hayt

Heinz Kluetmeier

Caryn Levy

Tony Tomsic

CHRISTOPHER LITTLE

WILL & DENI MCINTYRE

HARRY BENSON

ACEY HARPER

weekly

PHOTO & TEXT SYNDICATION EDITORIAL IMAGES

TIME & LIFE BUILDING
ROCKEFELLER CENTER
NY, NY 10020

212 522-2453
FAX 212 522-0884

CALL FOR

THE MON-TRÉSOR

–y–

CATALOG

1-800-356-3066

phototèque
MON·TRÉSOR

TOLL FREE 1–800–356–3066

FAX 1-312-427-0178   PHONE 1-312-427-8625

N S P

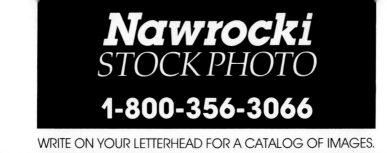

41

JEFF GNASS
P H O T O G R A P H Y

large

format

stock

photography

NaPali Coast

Colorado Rockies

Molokai Palms

Mount McKinley

Patagonia

P.O. BOX 91490 • PORTLAND, OR 97291-0490 • TEL 503/629-2020 • FAX 503/645-4931

COMSTOCK

COMSTOCK

© Comstock, Inc. 1992

In NY: 212.353.8600

Toll-Free: 800.225.2727   Fax: 212.353.3383

Comstock, Inc. 30 Irving Place New York 10003

France 36 Rue de Silly 92100 Boulogne TEL (1) 46 99 07 77 N° VERT (1) 05 25 27 27 FAX (1) 46 99 06 77

Germany Gottschedstrasse 4 W-1000 Berlin 65 TEL (030) 462 9090 SERVICE 130 855353 FAX (030) 462 9520

Canada 180 Bloor St. West Toronto M5S 2V6 TEL (416) 925 4323 TOLL-FREE (800) 387 0640 FAX (416) 964 8507

COMSTOCK

Free Catalog Available:
Call, Write, or Fax.

C O M S T O C K

In NY: 212.353.8600

Toll-Free: 800.225.2727   Fax: 212.353.3383

Comstock, Inc. 30 Irving Place New York 10003

France 36 Rue de Silly 92100 Boulogne TEL (1) 46 99 07 77 N° VERT (1) 05 25 27 27 FAX (1) 46 99 06 77

Germany Gottschedstrasse 4 W-1000 Berlin 65 TEL (030) 462 9090 SERVICE130 855353 FAX (030) 462 9520

Canada 180 Bloor St. West Toronto M5S 2V6 TEL (416) 925 4323 TOLL-FREE (800) 387 0640 FAX (416) 964 8507

COMSTOCK

Free Catalog Available:
Call, Write, or Fax.

COMSTOCK

In NY: 212.353.8600

Toll-Free: 800.225.2727

Fax: 212.353.3383

Comstock, Inc. 30 Irving Place New York 10003

France 36 Rue de Silly 92100 Boulogne TEL (1) 46 99 07 77 N° VERT (1) 05 25 27 27 FAX (1) 46 99 06 77

Germany Gottschedstrasse 4 W-1000 Berlin 65 TEL (030) 462 9090 SERVICE 130 855353 FAX (030) 462 9520

Canada 180 Bloor St. West Toronto M5S 2V6 TEL (416) 925 4323 TOLL-FREE (800) 387 0640 FAX (416) 964 8507

C O M S T O C K

Free Catalog Available:
Call, Write, or Fax.

COMSTOCK

© Comstock, Inc. 1992

In NY: 212.353.8600

Toll-Free: 800.225.2727   Fax: 212.353.3383

Comstock, Inc. 30 Irving Place New York 10003

France 36 Rue de Silly 92100 Boulogne TEL (1) 46 99 07 77 N° VERT (1) 05 25 27 27 FAX (1) 46 99 06 77

Germany Gottschedstrasse 4 W-1000 Berlin 65 TEL (030) 462 9090 SERVICE 130 855353 FAX (030) 462 9520

Canada 180 Bloor St. West Toronto M5S 2V6 TEL (416) 925 4323 TOLL-FREE (800) 387 0640 FAX (416) 964 8507

COMSTOCK

Free Catalog Available:
Call, Write, or Fax.

COMSTOCK

© Comstock, Inc. 1992

In NY: 212.353.8600
Toll-Free: 800.225.2727   Fax: 212.353.3383

Comstock, Inc. 30 Irving Place New York 10003

France 36 Rue de Silly 92100 Boulogne TEL (1) 46 99 07 77 N° VERT (1) 05 25 27 27 FAX (1) 46 99 06 77
Germany Gottschedstrasse 4 W-1000 Berlin 65 TEL (030) 462 9090 SERVICE 130 855353 FAX (030) 462 9520
Canada 180 Bloor St. West Toronto M5S 2V6 TEL (416) 925 4323 TOLL-FREE (800) 387 0640 FAX (416) 964 8507

COMSTOCK

Free Catalog Available:
Call, Write, or Fax.

Comstock, Inc. 30 Irving Place New York 10003

France 36 Rue de Silly 92100 Boulogne TEL (1) 46 99 07 77 N° VERT (1) 05 25 27 27 FAX (1) 46 99 06 77

Germany Gottschedstrasse 4 W-1000 Berlin 65 TEL (030) 462 9090 SERVICE 130 855353 FAX (030) 462 9520

Canada 180 Bloor St. West Toronto M5S 2V6 TEL (416) 925 4323 TOLL-FREE (800) 387 0640 FAX (416) 964 8507

53

COMSTOCK

© Comstock, Inc. 1992

In NY: 212.353.8600

Toll-Free: 800.225.2727   Fax: 212.353.3383

Comstock, Inc. 30 Irving Place New York 10003

France 36 Rue de Silly 92100 Boulogne TEL (1) 46 99 07 77 N° VERT (1) 05 25 27 27 FAX (1) 46 99 06 77

Germany Gottschedstrasse 4 W-1000 Berlin 65 TEL (030) 462 9090 SERVICE 130 855353 FAX (030) 462 9520

Canada 180 Bloor St. West Toronto M5S 2V6 TEL (416) 925 4323 TOLL-FREE (800) 387 0640 FAX (416) 964 8507

C O M S T O C K

Free Catalog Available:
Call, Write, or Fax.

COMSTOCK

In NY: 212.353.8600

Toll-Free: 800.225.2727   Fax: 212.353.3383

Comstock, Inc. 30 Irving Place New York 10003

France 36 Rue de Silly 92100 Boulogne TEL (1) 46 99 07 77 N° VERT (1) 05 25 27 27 FAX (1) 46 99 06 77

Germany Gottschedstrasse 4 W-1000 Berlin 65 TEL (030) 462 9090 SERVICE130 855353 FAX (030) 462 9520

Canada 180 Bloor St. West Toronto M5S 2V6 TEL (416) 925 4323 TOLL-FREE (800) 387 0640 FAX (416) 964 8507

COMSTOCK

Free Catalog Available:
Call, Write, or Fax.

Comstock, Inc. 30 Irving Place New York 10003

France 36 Rue de Silly 92100 Boulogne TEL (1) 46 99 07 77 N° VERT (1) 05 25 27 27 FAX (1) 46 99 06 77

Germany Gottschedstrasse 4 W-1000 Berlin 65 TEL (030) 462 9090 SERVICE 130 855353 FAX (030) 462 9520

Canada 180 Bloor St. West Toronto M5S 2V6 TEL (416) 925 4323 TOLL-FREE (800) 387 0640 FAX (416) 964 8507

COMSTOCK

© Comstock, Inc. 1992

In NY: 212.353.8600
Toll-Free: 800.225.2727   Fax: 212.353.3383

Comstock, Inc. 30 Irving Place New York 10003

France 36 Rue de Silly 92100 Boulogne TEL (1) 46 99 07 77 Nº VERT (1) 05 25 27 27 FAX (1) 46 99 06 77
Germany Gottschedstrasse 4 W-1000 Berlin 65 TEL (030) 462 9090 SERVICE130 855353 FAX (030) 462 9520
Canada 180 Bloor St. West Toronto M5S 2V6 TEL (416) 925 4323 TOLL-FREE (800) 387 0640 FAX (416) 964 8507

COMSTOCK

COMSTOCK

Free Catalog Available:
Call, Write, or Fax.

C O M S T O C K

© Comstock, Inc. 1992

In NY: 212.353.8600
Toll-Free: 800.225.2727   Fax: 212.353.3383

Comstock, Inc. 30 Irving Place New York 10003

France 36 Rue de Silly 92100 Boulogne TEL (1) 46 99 07 77 N° VERT (1) 05 25 27 27 FAX (1) 46 99 06 77

Germany Gottschedstrasse 4 W-1000 Berlin 65 TEL (030) 462 9090 SERVICE 130 855353 FAX (030) 462 9520

Canada 180 Bloor St. West Toronto M5S 2V6 TEL (416) 925 4323 TOLL-FREE (800) 387 0640 FAX (416) 964 8507

C O M S T O C K

COMSTOCK

© Comstock, Inc. 1992

In NY: 212.353.8600

Toll-Free: 800.225.2727   Fax: 212.353.3383

Comstock, Inc. 30 Irving Place New York 10003

France 36 Rue de Silly 92100 Boulogne TEL (1) 46 99 07 77   N° VERT (1) 05 25 27 27   FAX (1) 46 99 06 77

Germany Gottschedstrasse 4 W-1000 Berlin 65 TEL (030) 462 9090   SERVICE 130 855353   FAX (030) 462 9520

Canada 180 Bloor St. West Toronto M5S 2V6 TEL (416) 925 4323   TOLL-FREE (800) 387 0640   FAX (416) 964 8507

COMSTOCK

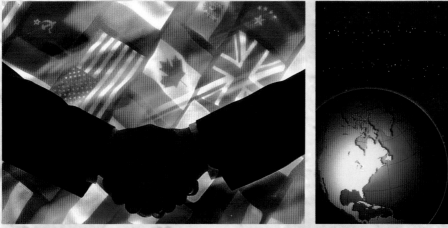

Free Catalog Available:
Call, Write, or Fax.

COMSTOCK

Berlin

Egypt

Paris

© Comstock, Inc. 1992

In NY: 212.353.8600

Toll-Free: 800.225.2727   Fax: 212.353.3383

Comstock,Inc. 30 Irving Place New York 10003

France 36 Rue de Silly 92100 Boulogne TEL (1) 46 99 07 77 N° VERT (1) 05 25 27 27 FAX (1) 46 99 06 77

Germany Gottschedstrasse 4 W-1000 Berlin 65 TEL (030) 462 9090 SERVICE130 855353 FAX (030) 462 9520

Canada 180 Bloor St. West Toronto M5S 2V6 TEL (416) 925 4323 TOLL-FREE (800) 387 0640 FAX (416) 964 8507

COMSTOCK

© Comstock, Inc. 1992

In NY: 212.353.8600
Toll-Free: 800.225.2727   Fax: 212.353.3383

Comstock, Inc. 30 Irving Place New York 10003

France 36 Rue de Silly 92100 Boulogne TEL (1) 46 99 07 77 N° VERT (1) 05 25 27 27 FAX (1) 46 99 06 77

Germany Gottschedstrasse 4 W-1000 Berlin 65 TEL (030) 462 9090 SERVICE130 855353 FAX (030) 462 9520

Canada 180 Bloor St. West Toronto M5S 2V6 TEL (416) 925 4323 TOLL-FREE (800) 387 0640 FAX (416) 964 8507

COMSTOCK

Free Catalog Available:
Call, Write, or Fax.

C O M S T O C K

© Comstock, Inc. 1992

In NY: 212.353.8600

Toll-Free: 800.225.2727   Fax: 212.353.3383

Comstock, Inc. 30 Irving Place New York 10003

France 36 Rue de Silly 92100 Boulogne TEL (1) 46 99 07 77 Nº VERT (1) 05 25 27 27 FAX (1) 46 99 06 77

Germany Gottschedstrasse 4 W-1000 Berlin 65 TEL (030) 462 9090 SERVICE 130 855353 FAX (030) 462 9520

Canada 180 Bloor St. West Toronto M5S 2V6 TEL (416) 925 4323 TOLL-FREE (800) 387 0640 FAX (416) 964 8507

COMSTOCK

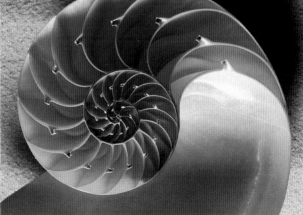

Free Catalog Available:
Call, Write, or Fax.

Comstock, Inc. 30 Irving Place New York 10003

France 36 Rue de Silly 92100 Boulogne TEL (1) 46 99 07 77 N° VERT (1) 05 25 27 27 FAX (1) 46 99 06 77

Germany Gottschedstrasse 4 W-1000 Berlin 65 TEL (030) 462 9090 SERVICE130 855353 FAX (030) 462 9520

Canada 180 Bloor St. West Toronto M5S 2V6 TEL (416) 925 4323 TOLL-FREE (800) 387 0640 FAX (416) 964 8507

COMSTOCK

AERIALS by WINGSTOCK ®

Coastal Santa Monica, California

In NY: 212.353.8600

Toll-Free: 800.225.2727   Fax: 212.353.3383

Comstock, Inc. 30 Irving Place New York 10003

France 36 Rue de Silly 92100 Boulogne TEL (1) 46 99 07 77 N° VERT (1) 05 25 27 27 FAX (1) 46 99 06 77

Germany Gottschedstrasse 4 W-1000 Berlin 65 TEL (030) 462 9090 SERVICE 130 855353 FAX (030) 462 9520

Canada 180 Bloor St. West Toronto M5S 2V6 TEL (416) 925 4323 TOLL-FREE (800) 387 0640 FAX (416) 964 8507

COMSTOCK
DESKTOP PHOTOGRAPHY™

Ask an Art Director what's the hardest photo to find and he'll answer, *"The one I want."*

© Comstock, Inc. 1992

In NY: 212.353.8600
Toll-Free: 800.225.2727   Fax: 212.353.3383

C O M S T O C K

D E S K T O P P H O T O G R A P H Y ™

Sure, it's subjective, and your choice has to please lots
of people. You probably feel you have to "see it all" and
with proliferating agencies and digital photo discs that's
hard to do. We can promise you this: More often than
not, you'll find that ONE at Comstock.

You'll also find millions of excellent commercial and
editorial photographs (besides the one you want); highly
skilled researchers to steer your quest, and customer
service that will bowl you over.

As a stock agency we are unsurpassed in
innovation. We've been offering digital imagery for
several years. Request transparencies or digital files:
The delivery method is up to you. But if you're design-
ing on computers, you'll find our images look as good
on your screen as they do on your lightbox.
And they work. Comstock photographers shoot
with your projects in mind.

Save time. Start your search at Comstock. The ONE.

For Information About
Comstock Desktop Photography™: Call, Write, or Fax.

Comstock, Inc. 30 Irving Place New York 10003

France 36 Rue de Silly 92100 Boulogne TEL (1) 46 99 07 77 N° VERT (1) 05 25 27 27 FAX (1) 46 99 06 77

Germany Gottschedstrasse 4 W-1000 Berlin 65 TEL (030) 462 9090 SERVICE 130 855353 FAX (030) 462 9520

Canada 180 Bloor St. West Toronto M5S 2V6 TEL (416) 925 4323 TOLL-FREE (800) 387 0640 FAX (416) 964 8507

The

Largest

and Most

Comprehensive

Automotive

Stock File

in the World

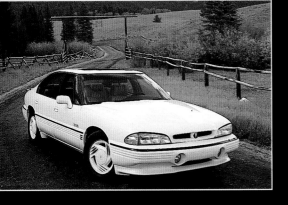

The
Largest
and Most
Comprehensive
Automotive
Stock File
in the World

FPG is both. Strikin

and evocative images tha

capture the past. Classic an

timeless images that conve

today. Past and presen

Then and now

Exceptional stock photograph

Available to you in just on

effortless call. For a free catalog

2 1 2 . 7 7 7 . 4 2 1 0 . Ope

8am to 8pm EST. **FPG**

THEN

AND

NOW

INTERNATIONAL

Jim Marshall

Bill Timmerman

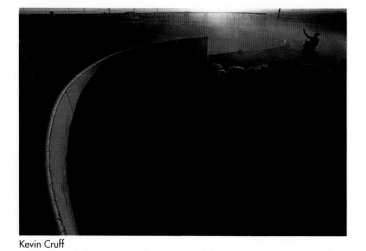

Kevin Cruff

Rick Raymond

Paul Loven

Scott Baxter

VISUAL IMAGES WEST, INC.

600 East Baseline #B6

Tempe, Arizona 85283-1210

IN ARIZONA 602-820-5403 / FAX 602-839-4014

1-800-433-4765

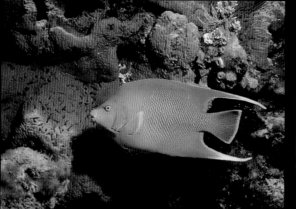

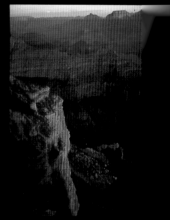

PHOTOGRAPHIC **RESOURCES**

STOCK photography + photographic **ART**

6633 Delmar
Saint Louis, Missouri 63130
TEL *314.721.5838*
FAX *314.721.0301*
TOLL FREE *1.800.933.5838*

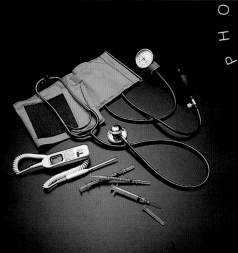

PHOTOGRAPHIC

RESOURCES

6633 Delmar
Saint Louis, Missouri 63130
TEL *314.721.5838*
FAX *314.721.0301*
TOLL FREE *1.800.933.5838*

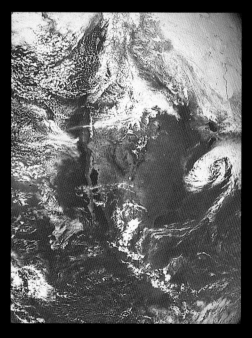

CURTIS MANAGEMENT GROUP
ENTERTAINMENT • SPORTS • ARTS • CORPORATE

Partial Client Listing

Entertainment
James Dean
Fred Astaire
Humphrey Bogart
James Cagney
Judy Garland
Edward G. Robinson
Errol Flynn
The Blues Brothers
Bud Abbott and Lou Costello
Johnny Weissmuller
William "Buckwheat" Thomas
Gordon "Porky" Lee
Thomas "Butch" Bond
Orson Welles

Will Rogers
Amelia Earhart
F. Scott Fitzgerald

Music
Buddy Holly
Hank Williams, Sr.
Billie Holiday
The Andrews Sisters

Olympians
Jesse Owens
Jim Thorpe

Football
Vince Lombardi
Paul Hornung
Bart Starr
Jim Taylor

Organizations
City of Beverly Hills
Hollywood Chamber of Commerce
Hollywood Walk of Fame
The Sporting News

Boxing
Joe Louis
Rocky Marciano
Joe Frazier
Jack Dempsey

Historical
Frank Lloyd Wright
Mark Twain

Basketball
Jerry Tarkanian
Bob Cousy

Baseball
Babe Ruth
Lou Gehrig
Cy Young
Honus Wagner
Ty Cobb
Billy Martin
Satchel Paige
Casey Stengel
Bob Feller
Whitey Ford
Eddie Mathews
Enos Slaughter
Johnny Mize
Harmon Killebrew

Curtis Management Group

**1000 Waterway Boulevard
Indianapolis, IN 46202
Telephone: (317) 633-2050
Telefax: (317) 633-2047**

Call us to discuss how you can include our clients in your next campaign or product line.

THE IMAGE BANK

In The

Beginning...

© ERIC MEOLA 426299

THE IMAGE BANK®

STOCK PHOTOGRAPHY, ILLUSTRATION AND FILM.

© JOE DEVENNEY 478802

© ROKUO KAWAKAMI 478801

© PETE TURNER 213106

THE IMAGE BANK

IMAGES FROM THE BEST TALENT IN THE WORLD.

© JOHN KELLY 212573

© STEVE SATUSHEK 213743

© JEAN MAHAUX 478805

THE IMAGE BANK®

OVER 5 MILLION IMAGES IN OUR LIBRARY.

© GEOFF GOLSON 752762

© JOHN WILLIAM BANAGAN 212019

© MICHAEL MELFORD 211825

© ALAN BECKER 478800

© DAVID DE LOSSY 02-0754-5941711

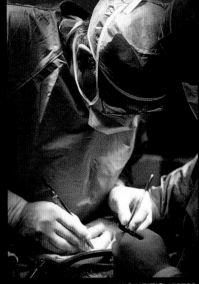

© ALVIS UPITIS 478799

© MICHAEL MELFORD 213619

© TERJE RAKKE 213388

© STEVEN HUNT 209843

© ERIC MEOLA 426283

THE IMAGE BANK

12 LOCATIONS IN THE UNITED STATES.

© LANCE LAVENSTEIN 1992

LavensteinStudios

PHOTOGRAPHY PRODUCTIONS & ADVERTISING

348 Southport Circle | Suite 103 | Virginia Beach, Virginia 23452 | 804.499.9959 | FAX: 804.499.9957

ACTION EMOTION HISTORY

POWER SPEED SPECTACLE

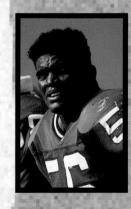

The Official Source For NFL Photography

NFL PHOTOS

6701 Center Drive West
Suite 1111
Los Angeles
California
90045

Telephone 310·215·1606
Fax 310·215·3813

800   487•4285
907 276•1343,   FAX: 907 258•7848
800 WEST 21ST AVE., ANCHORAGE, ALASKA 99503

© Daryl Pederson/ Extreme Skiing

© Myron Wright/ Mountains

© Johnny Johnson/ Hiker & Rainbow

© Johnny Johnson/ Eagle in Flight

© Alissa Crandall/ Walrus

© John Warden/ Bear & Cubs

© John Warden/ Mt. McKinley

© John Warden/ Wet Duck

© John Hyde/ Iceberg

© Randy Brandon/ Eskimo Girl

© Alissa Crandall/ Eagle Sunrise

907 276•1343,   FAX: 907 258•7848
800 WEST 21ST AVE., ANCHORAGE, ALASKA 99503

© Arend•Pinkerton/ Lake & Mountain Sunset

© Jeff Schultz/ Climber at Summit

© Mark Kelley/ Kayakers

© Jeff Schultz/ Grizzly Bear

© Alissa Crandall/ Eagle Landing

© Randy Brandon/ Sunset on Water

102

What If
Money Grew On Trees?

What If We Could
Cure Everything?

What If Chocolate Didn't
Have Any Calories?

What If Fish
Couldn't Swim?

What If SuperStock
Didn't Have It?

800-828-4545

Call or write for free catalogs.

New York: Tel (212) 633-0300 Fax (212) 633-0408   San Francisco: Tel (415) 781-4433 Fax (415) 781-8985

Sales representatives are located in 54 offices around the world. See the Affiliates Index for complete listing.

© 1992 SUPERSTOCK, INC.

★ Tel: 516 725 5100 Fax: 516 725 5159

Ressmeyer–Starlight, Inc., 179 North Side Drive, Sag Harbor, N.Y. 11963

RESSMEYER PHOTOGR★PHY

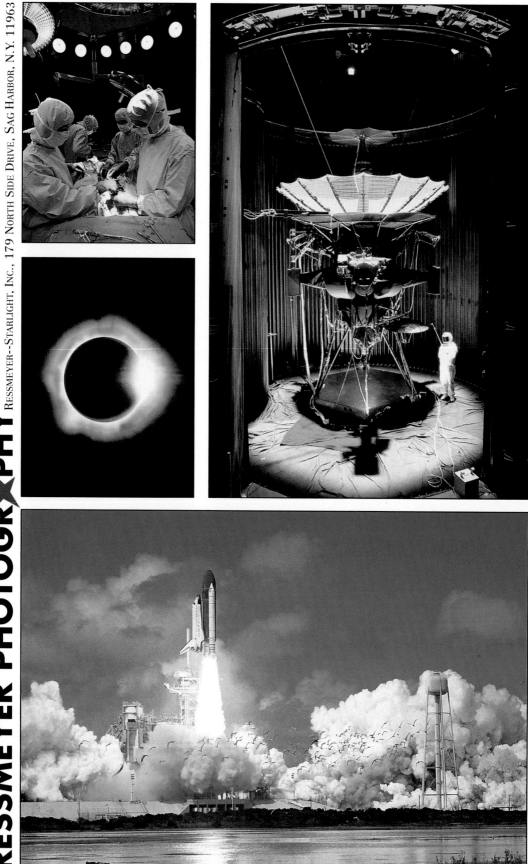

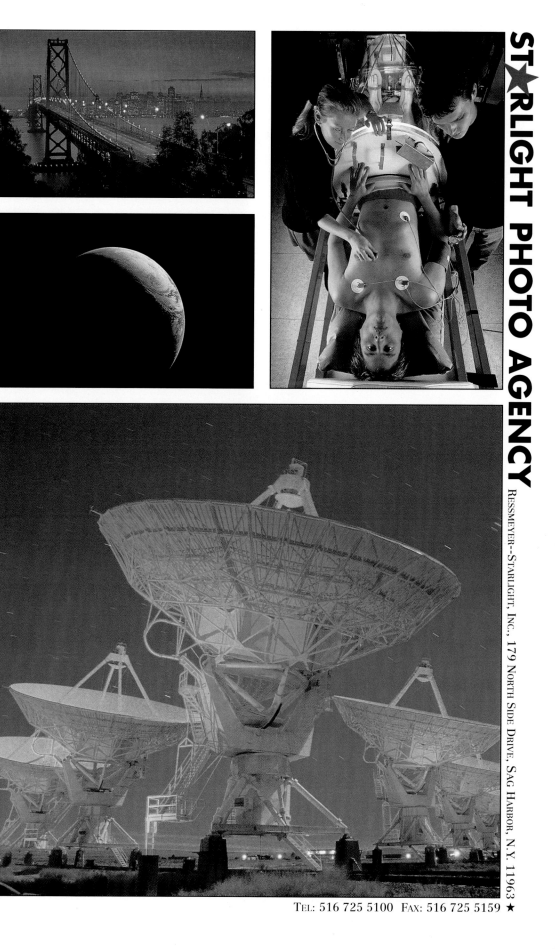

Bent photos.

The weird. The bizarre. The depraved. We've got it all. Some of the funniest historical stock money can rent.

Over 130,000 photos. In almost 1300 categories.

And for those without a sense of humor, we've also got that one of a kind historical stuff you'd expect to find in museums. Serious stuff. Wars, events, etc., etc.

So if you'd like our free brochure, or you have a specific category of photo in mind, give us a call.

Underwood Photo Archives. The stock house that's old and twisted.

UNDERWOOD PHOTO ARCHIVES
3109 Fillmore Street, San Francisco, CA 94123, (415) 346-2292

106

PETER ARNOLD

Peter Arnold, Inc.

B2001 Lion & Cub, Masai Mara, Kenya

© Yann Arthus-Bertrand

B2002 Cheetah, Masai Mara, Kenya

© Günter Ziesler

Peter Arnold, Inc.

B2003 Giraffes, Kenya

© Reinhard Künkel

1181 BROADWAY, NEW YORK, NY 10001   212/481-1190   FAX: 212-481-3409

800/289-7468

Peter Arnold, Inc.

B2004 Hands Holding Seedling

© Kelvin Aitken

B2005 Growth Rings of an Acacia Tree

© Manfred Kage

1181 BROADWAY, NEW YORK, NY 10001   212/481-1190   FAX: 212-481-3409

800/289-7468

Peter Arnold, Inc.

B2006   Midnight Sun, Arctic National Wildlife Refuge, Alaska

© Clyde H. Smith

1181 BROADWAY, NEW YORK, NY 10001   **212/481-1190**   **FAX: 212-481-3409**

800/289-7468

Peter Arnold, Inc.

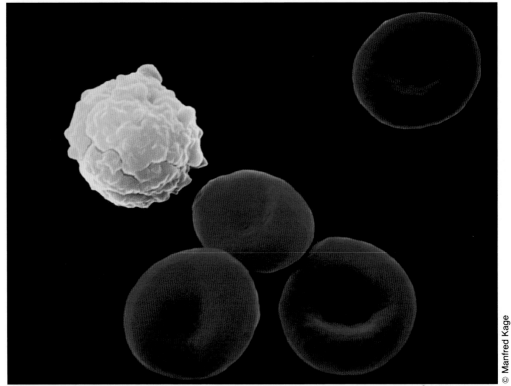

B2007   Human White & Red Blood Cells (SEM – 6250x)

© Manfred Kage

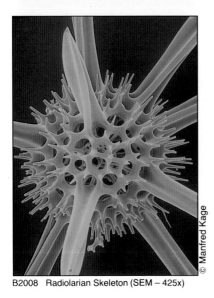

B2008   Radiolarian Skeleton (SEM – 425x)

© Manfred Kage

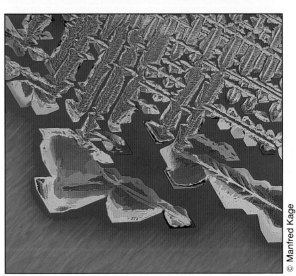

B2009   Sulfanilamide, Chemotherapy Drug (75x)

© Manfred Kage

1181 BROADWAY, NEW YORK, NY 10001   212/481-1190   FAX: 212-481-3409

800/289-7468

Peter Arnold, Inc.

B2010 Cat Flea (SEM – 100x)

Peter Arnold, Inc.

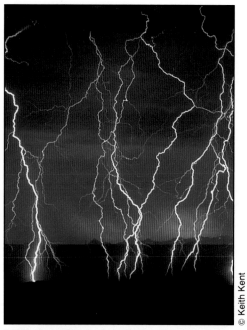

B2011   Desert Thunderstorm, Tucson, Arizona

© Keith Kent

B2012   Thunderstorm Over Tucson Foothills, Arizona

© Keith Kent

B2013   Summer Storm, Tucson, Arizona

© Keith Kent

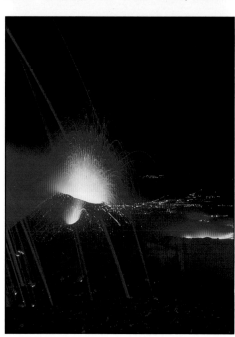

B2014   Night Eruption of Mt. Etna, Sicily

© Otto Hahn

1181 BROADWAY, NEW YORK, NY 10001   **212/481-1190**   **FAX: 212-481-3409**

800/289-7468

Peter Arnold, Inc.

B2015   Ripples on Water

© James H. Karales

B2016   Sandstone Slot Canyon, Arizona

© Art Twomey

B2017   Fair Weather Clouds

© Kevin Schafer

B2018   Clouds Building

© Werner H. Müller

B2019   Stratocumulus Clouds

© Kent Wood

1181 BROADWAY, NEW YORK, NY 10001   212/481-1190   FAX: 212-481-3409

800/289-7468

Peter Arnold, Inc.

B2020   School of Chromis Over Coral, Great Barrier Reef, Australia

© Fred Bavendam

© Fred Bavendam

B2021   Grouper, Red Sea

© Jeff Rotman

B2022   Four-Eye Butterfly Fish, South Caicos, BWI

1181 BROADWAY, NEW YORK, NY 10001   212/481-1190   FAX: 212-481-3409

800/289-7468

PACIFIC STOCK
Photography · Film · Video

© Greg Vaughn

© Four Eyes, Inc.

© Creative Focus

© William Waterfall

© Michael Howell

© Ed Robinson

© Bill Schildge

1-800-321

P.O. Box 90517 · Honolulu, HI 96835 · (808) 922-0975 · Fax:

OVER 5 MILLION IMAGES
FROM FACES, FAMOUS & INFAMOUS, TO HOLLYWOOD OLD & NEW.
FROM MOVIE STILLS AND HISTORICAL EVENTS TO PLACES AND LIFESTYLES.
PLUS A COMPREHENSIVE COLLECTION OF MODEL-RELEASED STOCK PHOTOS
COVERING AN ENCYCLOPEDIC RANGE OF SUBJECTS.
IN COLOR AND IN BLACK & WHITE.

CUSTOM MEDICAL STOCK PHOTO

3819 N. Southport
Chicago IL 60613-2823
phone 312.248.3200
fax 312.248.7427
800.373.2677

B.S.I.P.

34, RUE VILLIERS DE L'ISLE-ADAM
F-75020 PARIS, FRANCE
TEL 33.1.43.58.69.87
FAX 33.1.43.58.62.14

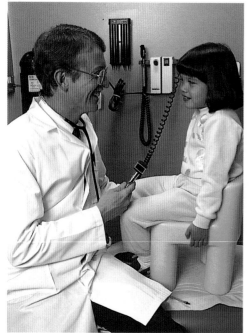

7102-T-1544, Pediatric Care

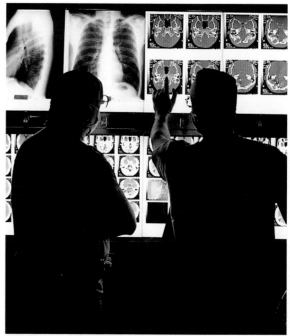

Z500-SS-3229, Radiologists. Consulting over radiographs, magnetic resonance and other imaging techniques.

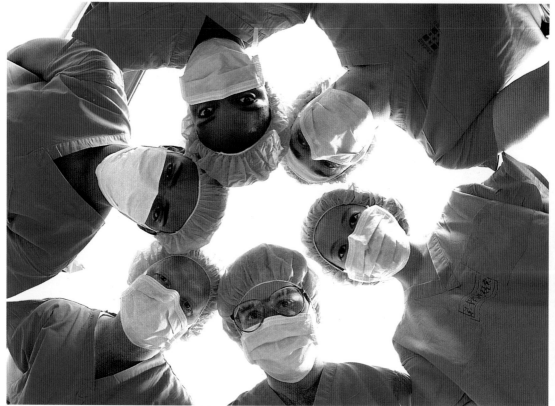

Z500-SS-2105, Healthcare Workers. Surgeons/Physicians in a circle, seen as if from the patient's view.

Specialists in Medical & Scientific Stock Photography

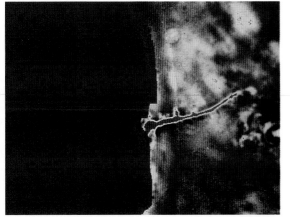

Z131-N-58, Conception. A single spermatozoon (human sperm) entering a human egg through the zona pellucida.

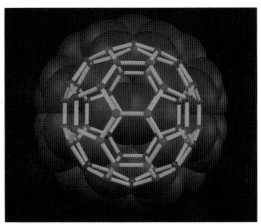

Z160-VV-51, Buckminsterfullerene, "Buckyball" Carbon-60 molecule. Computer graphic shows nuclei and bonds inside a transparent molecular surface.

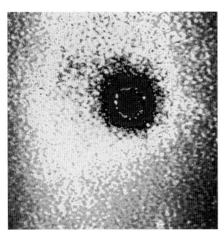

Z500-Q-8981, Rhinovirus. Scanning electron microscopy of the virus that causes the common cold.

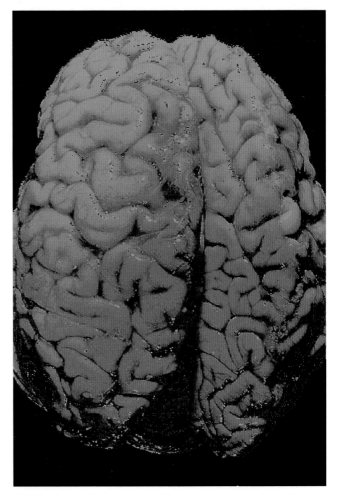

Z500-G-10695, Human Brain. Right and left cerebral hemispheres from above. Visible is the gyri and sulci. Highlighted in red is the longitudinal fissure and occipital pole.

Z775-A-114, Acaridae, mite. Itch mites produce many diseases in birds and mammals.

Specialists in Medical & Scientific Stock Photography

CUSTOM MEDICAL STOCK PHOTO

3819 N. Southport
Chicago IL 60613-2823
phone 312.248.3200
fax 312.248.7427
800.373.2677

B.S.I.P.

34, RUE VILLIERS DE L'ISLE-ADAM
F-75020 PARIS, FRANCE
TEL 33.1.43.58.69.87
FAX 33.1.43.58.62.14

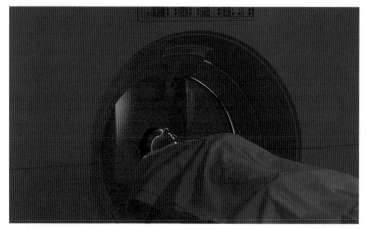

23h: Cat Scanner

NA26p:Blood Analysis

03a2: Consulting Geriatric Patient

AB94: Depression

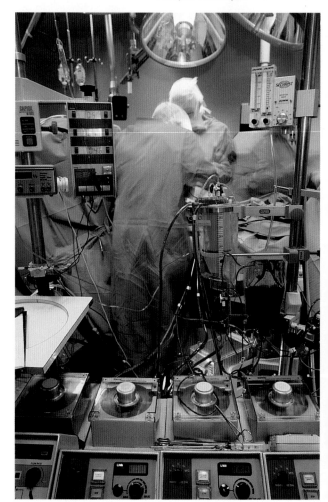

23h: Cardiac Transplant

Specialists in Medical & Scientific Stock Photography

CUSTOM MEDICAL STOCK PHOTO

3819 N. Southport
Chicago IL 60613-2823
phone 312.248.3200
fax 312.248.7427
800.373.2677

B.S.I.P.

34, RUE VILLIERS DE L'ISLE-ADAM
F-75020 PARIS, FRANCE
TEL 33.1.43.58.69.87
FAX 33.1.43.58.62.14

QB18w: Cancer Research: Killer Lymphocytes attacking a cancerous cell

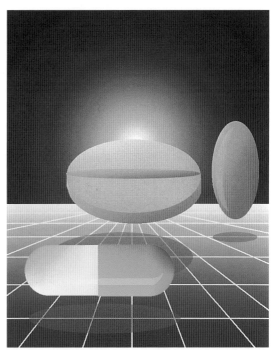

32-01: Pharmaceuticals

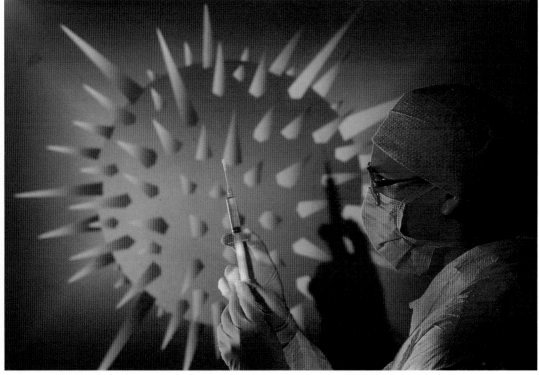

QB18w: Research for Aids Vaccine

Specialists in Medical & Scientific Stock Photography

iNSTOCK
PICTURE AGENCY

PETER LANGONE

NETWORK PRODUCTIONS

J. CHRISTOPHER

516 NORTHEAST 13TH STREET, FORT LAUDERDALE, FLORIDA 33304
(305) 527-4111   FAX # (305) 522-2562

POINT OF VIEW

TAKE IT VISUALLY

POINT OF VIEW BILDAGENTUR · ART-CONSULTING
HOFWEG 9 · D-2000 HAMBURG 76 · TELEFON 040/22 22 44 · FAX 040/48 20 20

© LONI LIEBERMANN

© HEROLD SHED

© STEFAN BÜCHNER

© STEFAN BÜCHNER

© ROBERT F. HAMMERSTIEL

© DIMITRI ENES

© ROBERT WERLING

© BEATE WEISSWANGE

129

SPORTS

DAVID MADISON

415-961-6297
FAX 415-967-1870

ARE YOU TIRED OF DEALING WITH PEOPLE WHO DON'T UNDERSTAND YOU?

At The Wildlife Collection, we specialize in nature. We've got the best chance of having what you want and knowing what you're talking about. We know tawny frogmouths aren't frogs, lizard cuckoos aren't reptiles, and cuttlefish aren't fish. And we have the photos to prove it!

Call us for our stunning scenics. Call us for our international rain forests and other worldwide vegetation. Call us for the best images of wildlife available in stock.

We are the only phone call you have to make when your photo needs run wild.

THE WILDLIFE COLLECTION

69 Cranberry Street, Brooklyn, NY 11201
(718)935-9600 • Fax (718)935-9031 • (800)373-5151
Open Monday–Friday, 8am–8pm.
Weekends by Appointment

THE STOCK MARKET

BB-P0035   Michael Keller

BB-CP0036   Dale O'Dell

BB-A0038   Chris Collins

BB-P0039   Claus Benser

BB-P0037   Claus Benser

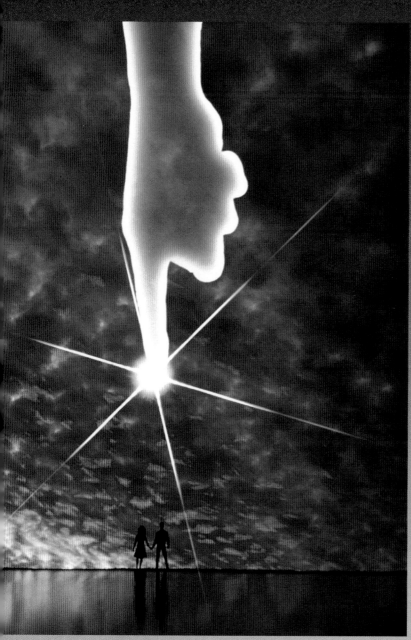

BB-P0040   Dale O'Dell

BB-P0041   Michael Keller

BB-P0042   Ronnie Kaufman

BB-P0045   Craig Hammell

BB-P0046   Michael Keller

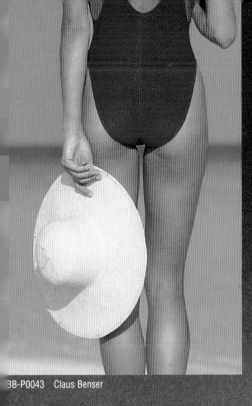

BB-P0043   Claus Benser

BB-P0044   Ronnie Kaufman

BB-P0047   Chris Collins

137

BB-M0048   Joe Towers   F/A 18D Hornet

BB-SP0049   Mallaun

BB-SP0051   Bezard

BB-SP0052   Bezard

BB-SP0050   Anne-Marie Weber

BB-SP0053   Schwertner

THE STOCK MARKET®
800-999-0800
(ALL STATES)

FAX HOTLINE
800-283-0808

139

BB-P0054   Jon Feingersh

BB-IN0055   Francesco Cascioli

BB-P0058   Michael Keller

BB-P0059   Michael Keller

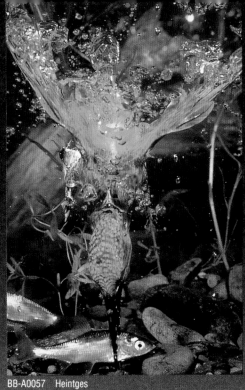

BB-C0056   Masahiro Sano

BB-A0057   Heintges

BB-F0060   Chris Collins

BB-B0061   Dale O'Dell

BB-B0062   Peter Garfield

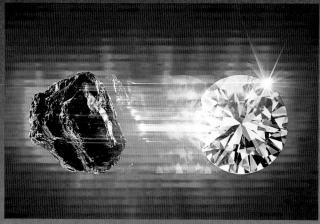

BB-IN0065   Myron J. Dorf

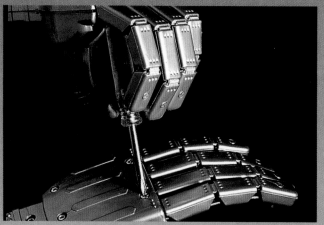

BB-IN0066   Craddock

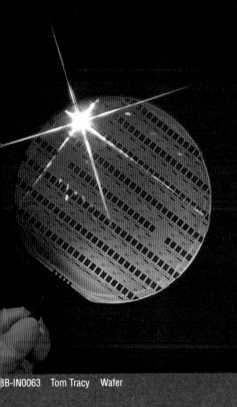

BB-IN0063 Tom Tracy Wafer

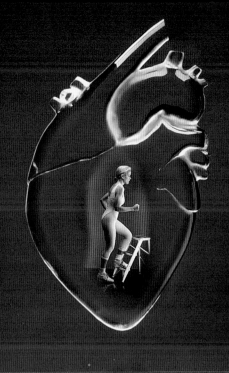

BB-SM0064 Ed Gallucci

BB-CP0067 Chris Collins

THE STOCK MARKET®

800-999-0800
(ALL STATES)

FAX HOTLINE
800-283-0808

143

BB-B0068   Masahiro Sano

STOCKNET®

SERVING THE WORLD

AMSTERDAM
ZEFA
TEL: (020) 661 38 66

BERLIN
CALL ZEFA DUSSELDORF
TEL: (0211) 5506-0 / 5506-1

BRUSSELS
BENELUX PRESS B.V.
TEL: (02) 7350772

COPENHAGEN
IFOT
TEL: 31386111

DUSSELDORF
ZEFA
TEL: (0211) 5506-0 / 5506-1

FRANKFURT
ZEFA FRANKFURT
TEL: (069) 75 80 4575

HAMBURG
ZEFA
TEL: (040) 4102083

HELSINKI
FINNISH PRESS AGENCY
TEL: (0) 15661

HONG KONG
STOCK HOUSE
TEL: (852) 866-0887

LEIPZIG
ZEFA LEIPZIG
TEL: (0037 41) 29 58 94

LISBON
AGENCIA DIAS DA SILVA
TEL: (1) 823217

LONDON
ZEFA PICTURE LIBRARY
TEL: (71) 262-0101 / 5

LYON
ZEFA FRANCE S.A.R.L.
TEL: (7) 8 92 87 66

MELBOURNE
STOCK PHOTOS
TEL: (3) 699-7600

MILAN
GRANATA PRESS SERVICE
TEL: (2) 26680702

MUNICH
CALL ZEFA DUSSELDORF
TEL: (0211) 5506-0 / 5506-1

OSLO
KUNDSEN
TEL: (02) 422831

PARIS
ZEFA FRANCE S.A.R.L.
TEL: (1) 42 74 55 47

ROME
SIE
TEL: (6) 3241681

STOCKHOLM
SJOEBERG PRESS SERVICE
TEL: (08) 99 92 63

SYDNEY
STOCK PHOTOS
TEL: (2) 954-3988

TEL AVIV
VISUAL PHOTO LIBRARY
TEL: (3) 546 3433

TOKYO
IMPERIAL PRESS
TEL: (3) 3585 2721

TORONTO
MASTERFILE
TEL: (416) 977-7267

WIEN
ZEFA
TEL: (0222) 327450

ZURICH
ZEFA
TEL: (01) 363 06 07

THE STOCK MARKET®

Stock Photography at Its Best

1-800-999-0800

ALL STATES

FAX 800-283-0808

Send For Our Free 176 Page Color Catalog

The Stock Market • 360 Park Avenue South, New York, NY 10010 • 212-684-7878

144

STOCK OPTIONS

Bill Van Calsem

Philip Gould

Sandra Russell Clark

Lloyd Poissenot

Bill Bachmann

Tom McCarthy

BLUE THUNDER PICTURES

SPECIALISTS
IN UNIQUE
HIGH QUALITY
MILITARY
IMAGES

CONTACT:
ANTONY PLATT
2350 BROADWAY
SUITE 825
NEW YORK CITY
1 0 0 2 4
TEL 212-496-0908

Photo Edit

David Young-Wolff

Tony Freeman

David Young-Wolff

Tony Freeman

Bill Stern

MINORITIES, SENIORS, TEENS, CHILDREN, FAMILIES

Mary Kate Denny

Michael Newman

Robert Brenner

Myrleen Ferguson

Alan Oddie

Felicia Martinez

PHOTO EDIT

6056 Corbin Avenue

Tarzana, CA 91356

TEL 818.342.2811

FAX 818.343.9548

151

CARR CLIFTON

891 GENESEE ROAD • TAYLORSVILLE, CA 95983 • 916/284-6205 • Fax: 916/284-7765

Independence Pass, CO

Big Sur, CA

Adirondacks, NY

Grand Tetons, WY

Antelope Valley, CA

Guadalupe Mountains, TX

LARGE FORMAT IMAGES FOR SUPERIOR DETAIL AND CLARITY

All Photos © Carr Clifton

CARR CLIFTON

891 GENESEE ROAD • TAYLORSVILLE, CA 95983 • 916/284-6205 • Fax: 916/284-7765

Salmon River, ID

Ansel Adams Wilderness, CA

Bob Marshall Wilderness, MT

Lake Superior, MN

Acadia National Park, ME

Anza Borrego, CA

LARGE FORMAT IMAGES FOR SUPERIOR DETAIL AND CLARITY

All Photos © Carr Clifton

FOCUS ON SPORTS, INC.

HANK AARON

WILLIE MAYS

TERRY BRADSHAW

REGGIE JACKSON

ALL-TIME ALL-STARS

ALL-TIME ALL-STARS

DICK BUTKUS

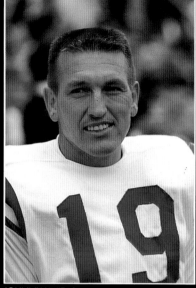

JOHNNY UNITAS

MICKEY MANTLE

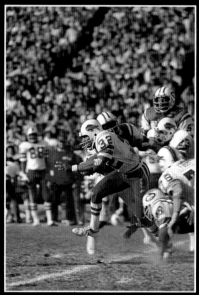

O.J. SIMPSON

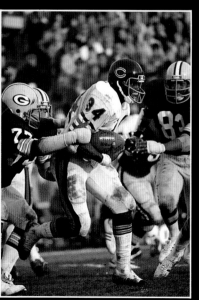

WALTER PAYTON

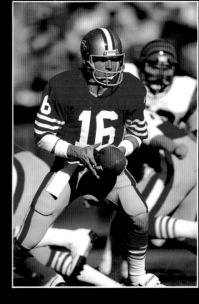

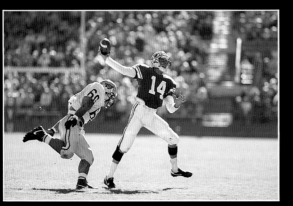

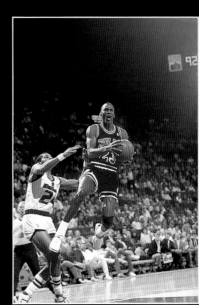

FOCUS
ON
SPORTS
INC.

PROFESSIONAL
SPORTS

FOCUS ON SPORTS, INC.

LEISURE & COMPETITIVE SPORTS

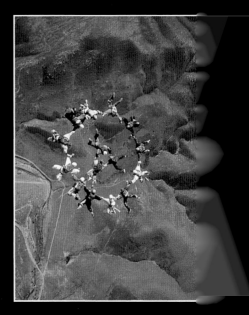

PROFILES WEST

210 E. Main, P.O. Box 1199

Buena Vista, Colorado 81211

TEL 719.395.8671 / FAX 719.395.8840

Wiley/Wales

Allen Russell

Phil Lauro

P. Barry Levy

Jack Hoehn Jr.

Bob Winsett

WHEN YOU WANT THE WEST,
COME TO THE WEST.

WHILE YOU'RE HERE, WE'LL ALSO
GIVE YOU THE WORLD.

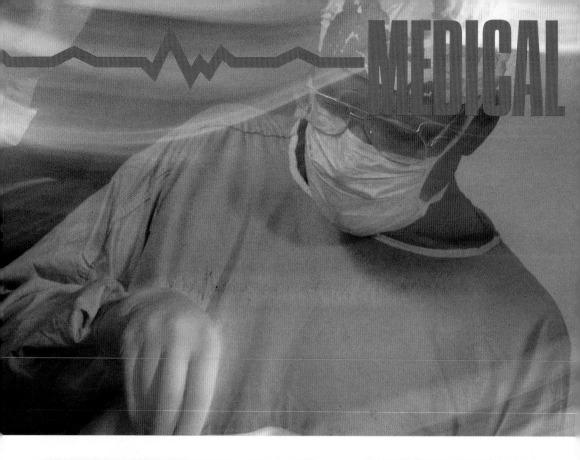

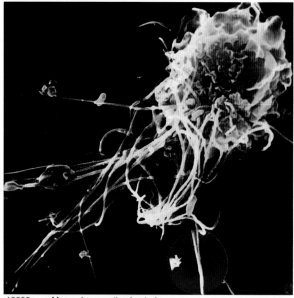

13600   Macrophage eating bacteria

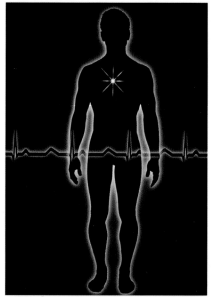

26091

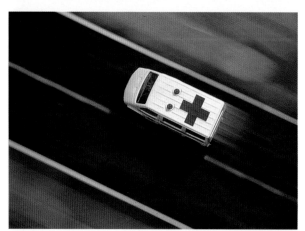

26110

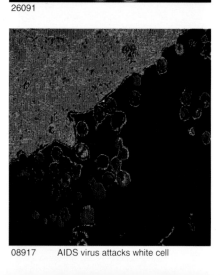

08917   AIDS virus attacks white cell

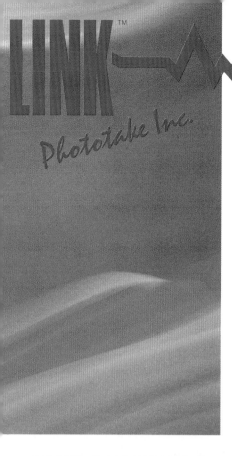
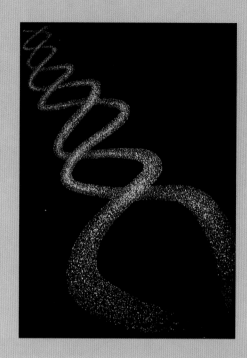

SHARPSHOOTERS

Sharpshooters
(800) 666-1266
Fax (305) 666-5485

Dusseldorf ZEFA
(02 11) 55 06-0

Frankfurt ZEFA
(0 69) 75 80 45 75

Hamburg ZEFA
(0 40) 4 10 20 83

Wien ZEFA
(02 22) 32 74 50

Amsterdam ZEFA
(0 20) 66 138 66

**UK ZEFA
Picture Library**
(01) 262 0101

RANDY MILLER

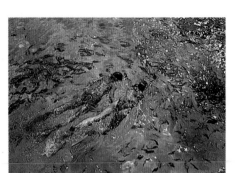

GARY KUFNER

RICK DIAZ

HUGHES MARTIN

PREMIUM STOCK PHOTOGRAPHY

1-800-666-1266
USA & Canada

HUGHES MARTIN

JERRY TOBIAS

HUGHES MARTIN

GARY KUFNER

RANDY MILLER

Sharpshooters
(800) 666-1266
Fax (305) 666-5485

Dusseldorf ZEFA
(02 11) 55 06-0

Frankfurt ZEFA
(0 69) 75 80 45 75

Hamburg ZEFA
(0 40) 4 10 20 83

Wien ZEFA
(02 22) 32 74 50

Amsterdam ZEFA
(0 20) 66 138 66

UK ZEFA
Picture Library
(01) 262 0101

PREMIUM STOCK PHOTOGRAPHY

1-800-666-1266
USA & Canada

aris ZEFA
) 42 74 55 47

Lyon ZEFA
(07) 78 92 87 66

Milano ZEFA
(02) 48 00 45 25

Zurich ZEFA
(01) 3 63 06 07

Stockholm,
Sjoberg Press Service
(08) 999 263

Melbourne, Australia
Auschromes Pty Ltd.
(03) 613 699 3222

Tokyo,
Imperial Press
81-3-3585-2721

169

Sharpshooters
(800) 666-1266
Fax (305) 666-5485

Dusseldorf ZEFA
(02 11) 55 06-0

Frankfurt ZEFA
(0 69) 75 80 45 75

Hamburg ZEFA
(0 40) 4 10 20 83

Wien ZEFA
(02 22) 32 74 50

Amsterdam ZEFA
(0 20) 66 138 66

UK ZEFA
Picture Library
(01) 262 0101

RANDY MILLER

BOB GELBERG

RANDY MILLER

MATT MILLER

RAOUL MINSART

SHARPSHOOTERS™

PREMIUM STOCK PHOTOGRAPHY

1-800-666-1266
USA & Canada

PAUL MORRIS

BOB GELBERG

GARY KUFNER

GARY KUFNER

Sharpshooters
(800) 666-1266
Fax (305) 666-5485

Dusseldorf ZEFA
(02 11) 55 06-0

Frankfurt ZEFA
(0 69) 75 80 45 75

Hamburg ZEFA
(0 40) 4 10 20 83

Wien ZEFA
(02 22) 32 74 50

Amsterdam ZEFA
(0 20) 66 138 66

**UK ZEFA
Picture Librar**
(01) 262 0101

DAVID HALL

S H A R P / S / H O O T E R S ™

PREMIUM STOCK PHOTOGRAPHY

1-800-666-1266
USA & Canada

Paris ZEFA
(1) 42 74 55 47

Lyon ZEFA
(07) 78 92 87 66

Milano ZEFA
(02) 48 00 45 25

Zurich ZEFA
(01) 3 63 06 07

**Stockholm,
Sjoberg Press Service**
(08) 999 263

**Melbourne, Australia
Auschromes Pty Ltd.**
(03) 613 699 3222

**Tokyo,
Imperial Press**
81-3-3585-2721

173

Tom & Pat Leeson

Vancouver, Washington

(206) 256-0436

Specializing in North American wildlife, including many rare and endangered species.

What If
You Could Walk On Water?

What If New York Didn't Have A Skyline?

What If There Were Golden Geese?

What If Grass Wasn't Green?

What If SuperStock Didn't Have It?

SUPERSTOCK
FOUR BY FIVE

800-828-4545

Call or write for free catalogs.

New York: Tel (212) 633-0300 Fax (212) 633-0408   San Francisco: Tel (415) 781-4433 Fax (415) 781-8985

Sales representatives are located in 54 offices around the world. See the Affiliates Index for complete listing.

al Accident, 1928

ddy Marvelous, Eton 1954

onation of King George VI, 1937

The Little Refugee

Shoot for the best.
With over 20 years experience,
we are one of the largest stock agencies in Japan.
We may be large,
but the key to our success is personalized service.
We never forget the importance of our overseas photographers.
Shoot for Camera Tokyo Service.

CAMERA TOKYO SERVICE CO.,LTD.
6F Park Heights 6-31-17, Jingumae, Shibuya-ku, Tokyo, Japan.
tel. 81-3-3407-7181 fax. 81-3-3400-7734

SHOOT F

OR JAPAN

Nawrocki STOCK PHOTO

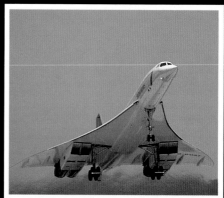

THIRD COAST STOCK SOURCE

CALL THE COAST FOR
WORLDWIDE TRAVEL

PHOTO REQUESTS: 1.800.323.9337

PO BOX 92397, MILWAUKEE, WI USA 53202, TEL 414.765.9442, FAX 414.765.9342

THE BACKGROUND FILE™

IS YOUR BACKGROUND SOURCE AT THE COAST

THE
MIDWEST
ROCK PHOTO
AGENCY

PHOTO REQUESTS: 1.800.323.9337

PO BOX 92397, MILWAUKEE, WI USA 53202, TEL 414.765.9442, FAX 414.765.9342

CALL THE COAST FOR IMAGES OF

BUSINESS

CALL THE COAST FOR IMAGES OF
INDUSTRY

PHOTO REQUESTS: 1.800.323.9337

PO BOX 92397, MILWAUKEE, WI USA 53202, TEL 414.765.9442, FAX 414.765.9342

THE
MIDWEST
STOCK PHO
AGENCY

CLASSICS

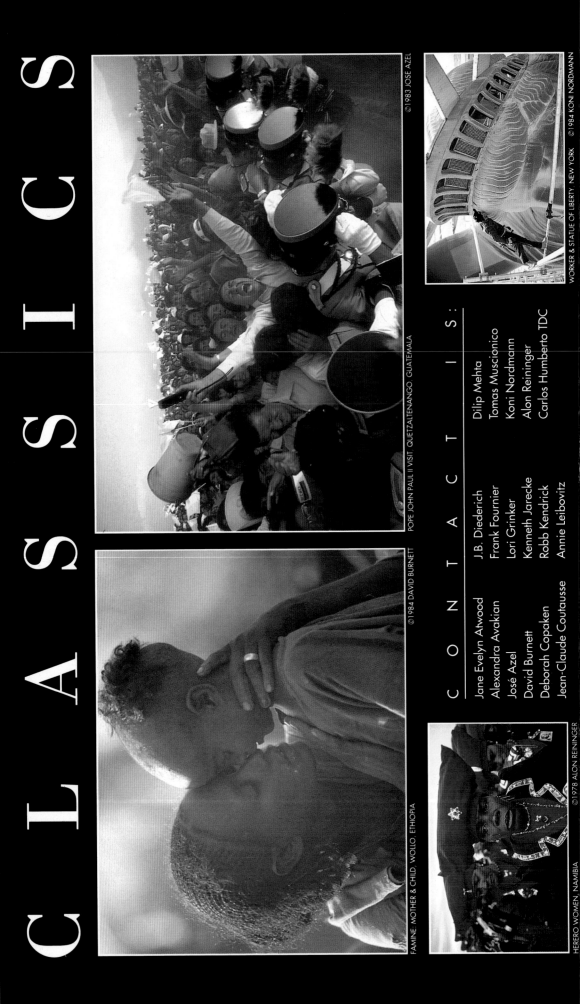

© 1983 JOSÉ AZEL

POPE JOHN PAUL II VISIT, QUETZALTENANGO, GUATEMALA

© 1984 DAVID BURNETT

WORKER & STATUE OF LIBERTY, NEW YORK

© 1984 KONI NORDMANN

FAMINE: MOTHER & CHILD, WOLLO, ETHIOPIA

HERERO WOMEN, NAMIBIA

© 1978 ALON REININGER

CONTACTS:

Jane Evelyn Atwood
Alexandra Avakian
José Azel
David Burnett
Deborah Copaken
Jean-Claude Coutausse

J.B. Diederich
Frank Fournier
Lori Grinker
Kenneth Jarecke
Robb Kendrick
Annie Leibovitz

Dilip Mehta
Tomas Muscionico
Koni Nordmann
Alon Reininger
Carlos Humberto TDC

CLASSICS TO BE

PERFORMING PANDA, SHANGHAI, CHINA   ©1985 ALON REININGER

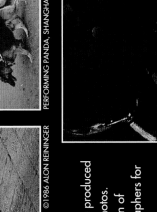

FOUNDRY WORKER, JUAREZ, MEXICO   ©1983 JOSÉ AZEL

OLD CITY, JERUSALEM, ISRAEL   ©1986 ALON REININGER

In the last decade, CONTACT photographers have produced some of the world's most memorable news photos. Now, CONTACT is proud to offer a selection of extraordinary stock images by the same photographers for advertising and other commercial uses.

CONTACT PRESS IMAGES INC

CONTACT PRESS IMAGES/USA: 116 EAST 27TH STREET, NEW YORK, NY USA 10016
TEL 212-481-6910, FAX 212-481-6909

CONTACT PRESS IMAGES/EUROPE: 104-106 RUE OBERKAMPF, PARIS, 75011 FRANCE
TEL 011-33-1-43-57-40-00, FAX 011-33-1-43-57-01-24

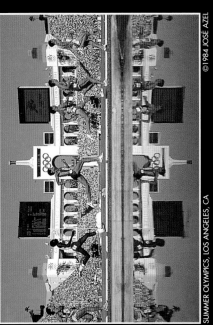

SUMMER OLYMPICS, LOS ANGELES, CA   ©1984 JOSÉ AZEL

AMAZON FOREST FIRE, RONDONIA, BRAZIL   ©1988 CARLOS HUMBERTO TDC

WaterHouse
STOCK PHOTOGRAPHY

Your single best source for…

Tropical Lifestyle

Marine Life

Sharks

Reef Scenics

Dive Adventure

Ecology Issues

Shipwrecks

Water Sports

800-451-3737
P.O. BOX 2487 • MILE MARKER 102.5 • KEY LARGO, FLORIDA 33037
FAX 305-451-5147

ALLSTOCK

·ALLSTOCK·

David Muench/Climber, Colorado #DM-X5910-111

Karl Weatherly/Kayaker #797231

Karl Weatherly/Climber #797232

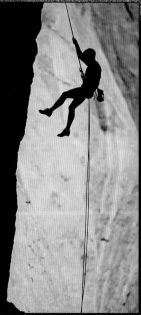

1-800-248-8116   206-622-6262   FAX 206-622-6662

·ALLSTOCK·

Tim Davis/Taking The Plunge #788602

·AllStock·

Darrell Jones/Big Waves, Hawaii #781364

Gary Moon/Vernal Falls, Yosemite #790989

1-800-248-8116   206-622-6262   FAX 206-622-6662

· ALLSTOCK ·

Larry Gilpin/Shock Waves #797517

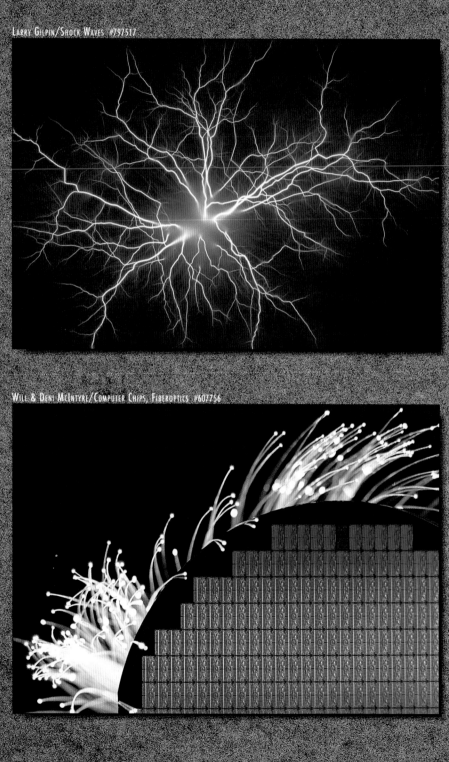

Will & Deni McIntyre/Computer Chips, Fiberoptics #607756

·ALLSTOCK·

Richard Kaylin/Lightning #701557

Richard Kaylin/Bay Area Storm #777684

1-800-248-8116   206-622-6262   FAX 206-622-6662

Joe Sohm/Tickertape Parade #297525

·ALLSTOCK·

Louis Bencze/Grinder #655631

Walter Hodges/Trucking #797516

Gary Holscher/Irrigation #797515

1-800-248-8116   206-622-6262   FAX 206-622-6662

·ALLSTOCK·

Fabricius & Taylor/Agreement #797527

Deni McIntyre/Waiting In Lobby #635680

David Muench/Redwoods #DM-F5569-1877

David Muench/White Mesa Arch #DM-F5570-1878

Liz Hymans/Grand Canyon #797512

Liz Hymans/Jasper #797514

Liz Hymans/Juneau Icefield #797513

Liz Hymans/Grand Canyon #797530

1-800-248-8116   206-622-6262   FAX 206-622-6662

·ALLSTOCK·

TIM THOMPSON/CAPE SPEAR #777299

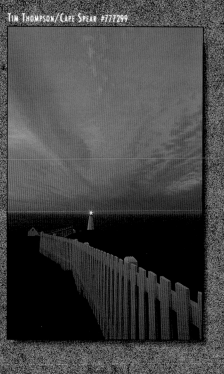

NICK GUNDERSON/MT. OLYMPUS #766179

JAMES MARTIN/NORTH CASCADES #797521

STUART WESTMORLAND/HECETA HEAD #730163

1-800-248-8116   206-622-6262   FAX 206-622-6662

213

· **ALLSTOCK** ·

DARRELL JONES/FLORIDA KEYS #1000108

DARRELL JONES/SAILFISH #781365

FABRICIUS & TAYLOR/ON VACATION! #1000479

DARRELL JONES/BAHAMAS #797518

· **ALLSTOCK** ·

BERT SAGARA/CABO SAN LUCAS #787297

BERT SAGARA/POSTCARDS #781291

BERT SAGARA/ADOBE, MEXICO #781287

BERT SAGARA/POOL, MEXICO #781290

1-800-248-8116   206-622-6262   FAX 206-622-6662

·ALLSTOCK·

Randy Wells/Kimonos #1000482

Kevin Morris/Umbrellas #797523   Dewitt Jones/Pacific Rim Business #797524

·ALLSTOCK·

Dewitt Jones/Businessmen, Japan (Released) #1000483

Fabricius & Taylor/Mother and Daughter #1000480

RSI/Walking The Dog #RS-023590-1

1-800-248-8116   206-622-6262   FAX 206-622-6662

·ALLSTOCK·

KEVIN MORRIS/BUBBLES #797529

RANDY TAYLOR/FUTURE PLANS #797528

RANDY TAYLOR/MOTHERHOOD #789941

1-800-248-8116   206-622-6262   FAX 206-622-6662

·ALLSTOCK·

ALASKA PHOTO COLLECTION

·ALLSTOCK·

ALASKA PHOTO COLLECTION

CHRIS NOBLE/CAMP, CHUGACH MOUNTAINS #114714

MARC MUENCH/BAGLEY ICE FIELD #MM-1019

·ALLSTOCK·

ALASKAPHOTO COLLECTION

FRED FELLEMAN/WHALE, PRINCE WILLIAM SOUND #111487

GREG PROBST/PRINCE WILLIAM SOUND #112756

JOHNNY JOHNSON/NORTHERN LIGHTS #104969

1-800-248-8116   206-622-6262   FAX 206-622-6662

·ALLSTOCK·
ALASKAPHOTO COLLECTION

Brian Stablyk/Midnight Sun #112863

Ken Graham/Oil Platform, Alaska #110486

1-800-248-8116   206-622-6262   FAX 206-622-6662

223

·ALLSTOCK·

AlaskaPhoto Collection

Johnny Johnson/Dall Sheep, Denali #73760

Johnny Johnson/Caribou #61806

Johnny Johnson/Grizzly Bears #820990

·ALLSTOCK·

ALASKAPHOTO COLLECTION

JOHNNY JOHNSON/ALASKA CAMPSITE #114715

ALAN HICKS/ALASKA NATIVES #114718

TIM THOMPSON/ESKIMO GIRL #394140

ROD CURRIE/WILDERNESS CABIN #772613

1-800-248-8116   206-622-6262   FAX 206-622-6662

· ALLSTOCK ·

ALASKAPHOTO COLLECTION

TOM BEAN/EAGLE ON ICEBERG #84904

JIM BOEDER/BERING SEA (RELEASED) #103110   NANCY SIMMERMAN/PORTAGE GLACIER #TB418

Art Wolfe/Kayak, Glacier #114716

·ALLSTOCK·

ANIMALS FOR ADVERTISING COLLECTION

ART WOLFE/LION DUET #832674

TIM DAVIS/LION #833270

TIM DAVIS/LION #833190

·ALLSTOCK·

ANIMALS FOR ADVERTISING COLLECTION

TIM DAVIS/TIGER #833161

·ALLSTOCK·

ANIMALS FOR ADVERTISING COLLECTION

ART WOLFE/SEE NO EVIL #832460

ART WOLFE/HEAR NO EVIL #832458

ART WOLFE/SPEAK NO EVIL #832449

ART WOLFE/CHIMPANZEE #832455

1-800-248-8116   206-622-6262   FAX 206-622-6662

·ALLSTOCK·

ANIMALS FOR ADVERTISING COLLECTION

THOMAS PETERSON/PARTY ANIMAL #834300

WILLIAM CURTSINGER/HARP SEAL PUP #PR-2738

ART WOLFE/HUMPBACK WHALE #834744

·ALLSTOCK·
ANIMALS FOR ADVERTISING COLLECTION

FRANS LANTING/KING PENGUINS #821031

KEVIN SCHAFER/EMPEROR PENGUINS #803865

Boston · Frank Siteman

Larry Lawfer

Frank Siteman

Barcelona · Michael J. Howell

c. 1920 · R.P. Kingston Collection

John Yurka

Folding camera c. 1920 · R.P. Kingston Collection

D. D. Morrison

the picture cube

Phone: 617·367·1532   **FAX: 617·482·9266**

The Picture Cube · 89 Broad Street · Boston, Massachusetts 02110

Exceptional Color and B&W Photography from New England and Around the World

© 1992 The Picture Cube, Inc.

John Coletti

Thailand · Sally Cassidy

African family c. 1880 · R.P. Kingston Collection

Frank Siteman

Kindra Clineff

Tony Mendoza

John Coletti

Ice man c. 1900 · R.P. Kingston Collection

PANORAMIC PHOTOGRAPHY
FROM THE MIDWEST TO THE FAR EAST

We are pleased to announce that we are now representing
Mon-Trésor, the Japanese source for
panoramic photography.

Write or fax for our new W catalogs.

パノラマ写真
アメリカ中西部から極東地域まで

モントレをご紹介します。パラノマ写真のアーティスティックな展開 — 日本から。

新しいWカタログをご希望の方は、電話、またはファクスでお申し込みください。

PANORAMIC IMAGES

WIDE
WIDER
WIDEST

230 N. MICHIGAN
CHICAGO, IL 60601

312-236-8545
FAX 312-704-4077

photothèque
MON·TRÉSOR

800-543-5250

PICTURE PERFECT USA, Inc.

. . . watching the future

BRINGING THE BEST IN STOCK PHOTOGRAPHY TO YOU.

CHARLES BOWMAN

ICL/PR

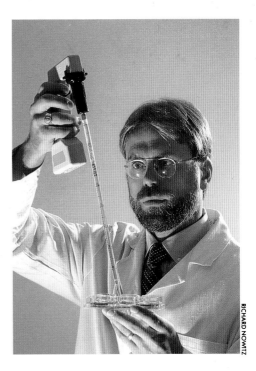

RICHARD NOWITZ

FREE COLOR CATALOG AVAILABLE

(212) 765-1212   Fax: (212) 765-1163
(800) 241-4477

Sports Chrome
East/West

IN SPORTS PHOTOGRAPHY, WE'RE IN A LEAGUE BY OURSELVES!

Professional • Collegiate • Amateur • Olympic Events • Adventure • Leisure • Health • Fitness

Ask about our extensive library of model-released images

IN THE EAST

Contact: Joyce Mead

10 Brinkerhoff Ave, Palisades Park, NJ 07650

Tel (201) 568-1412 • Fax (201) 944-1045

IN THE WEST

Contact: Tracey Prever

38 Quail Court, Walnut Creek, CA 94596

Tel (415) 398-7148 • Fax (510) 256-7754

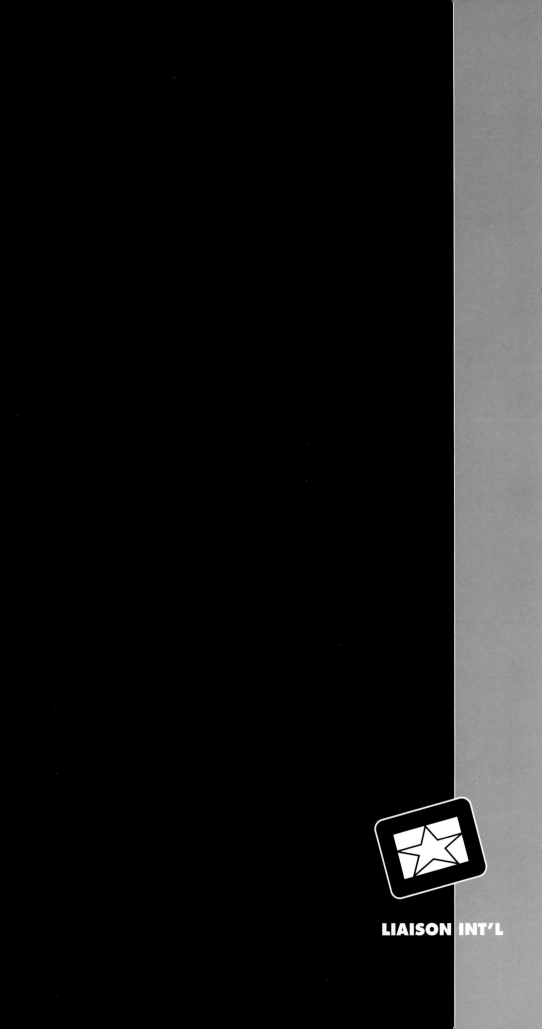

LIAISON INT'L

And Now, The White Book

Liaison International introduces The White Book—the stock catalogue conceived with

1

S T O C K

the designer and art director in mind. The White Book offers a selection of great existin

N119

N195

N159

N202

N110

N244

T103

T154

T120

T136

T134

T171

or other visual noise. The White Book reflects only a fragment of the Liaison Internationa

P104

P113

P121

P163

P105

P130

P129

S111

S116

S119

S141

S106

S124

and a full selection of slides will be shipped to you that same day. We can even send yo

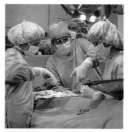

I289

I305

T182

F119

The White Book is a trademark of Liaison International, a Division of Liaison Agency, Inc., 11 E. 26 St., New York, NY 10010.

F132

M116

Call for a complete list of our foreign agents.

custom-created VHS videocassette with a larger choice for you to make your own edit.

I139

I226

I183

I153

I245

I239

I200

To order your copy of the Liaison International stock catalogue, or to initiate an image search, please give us a call at (800) 488-0844, or if you're calling from New York (212) 447-2509, or fax your layout to (212) 447-2534.

S T O C K *imagery*

To
order your
copy of our
1992 catalog, just call
and ask for the
In it, you'll discover a sparkling
source of rare and priceless images just
waiting to be discovered. Stock
Imagery®–Where Images
Connect™–with
you.

•

S T O C K *imagery*

Where Images Connect™

711 Kalamath Street, Denver, Colorado 80204

Steve Whalen

Lindy Powers

Ben Blankenburg

Craig Nelson

John Kieffer

303.592.1091   800.288.3686   Fax 303.592.1278

What If
There Were No Taxes?

What If Kids
Didn't Play?

What If There
Were No Art?

What If The 50s
Never Existed?

What If SuperStock
Didn't Have It?

AFFILIATE INDEX

DIALING INTERNATIONALLY

When dialing a European country, dial the international access code (below), drop the initial "0" of the phone number ("9" for Finland), then dial the remainder of the number.

TO (YOU WANT TO CALL) ▶
FROM (YOU ARE IN) ▶

FROM \ TO	Austria	Belgium	Canada	Denmark	Finland	France	Germany	Gr. Britain	Greece	Ireland	Italy	Japan	Netherlands	Norway	Portugal	Spain	Sweden	Switzerland	USA
Austria	–	0032	001	0045	00358	0033	06	0044	0030	00353	040	90081	0031	0047	00351	0034	0046	050	001
Belgium	0043	–	001	0045	00358	0033	0049	0044	0030	00353	0039	0081	0031	0047	00351	0034	0046	0041	001
Canada	01143	01132	–	01145	011358	01133	01149	01144	01130	011353	01139	01181	01131	01147	011351	01134	01146	01141	1
Denmark	00943	00932	0091	–	009358	00933	00949	00944	00930	009353	00939	00981	00931	00947	009351	00934	00946	00941	0091
Finland	99043	99032	9901	99045	–	99033	99049	99044	99030	990353	99039	99081	99031	99047	990351	99034	99046	99041	9901
France	1943	1932	191	1945	19358	–	1949	1944	1930	19353	1939	1981	1931	1947	19351	1934	1946	1941	191
Germany	0043	0032	001	0045	00358	0033	–	0044	0030	00353	0039	0081	0031	0047	00351	0034	0046	0041	001
Gr. Britain	01043	01032	0101	01045	010358	01033	01049	–	01030	0001	01039	01081	01031	01047	010351	01034	01046	01041	0101
Greece	0043	0032	001	0045	00358	0033	0049	0044	–	00353	0039	0081	0031	0047	00351	0034	0046	0041	001
Ireland	1643	1632	161	1645	16358	1633	1649	03	1630	–	1639	1681	1631	1647	16351	1634	1646	1641	161
Italy	0043	0032	001	0045	00358	0033	0049	0044	0030	00353	–	0081	0031	0047	00351	0034	0046	0041	001
Japan	00143	00132	0011	00145	001358	00133	00149	00144	00130	001353	00139	–	00131	00147	001351	00134	00146	00141	0011
Netherlands	0943	0932	091	0945	09358	0933	0949	0944	0930	09353	0939	0981	–	0947	09351	0934	0946	0941	091
Norway	09543	09532	0951	09545	095358	09533	09549	09544	09530	095353	09539	09581	09531	–	095351	09534	09546	09541	0951
Portugal	0743	0732	071	0745	07358	0733	0749	0744	0730	07353	0739	09781	0731	0747	–	0734	0746	0041	0971
Spain	0743	0732	071	0745	07358	0733	0749	0744	0730	07353	0739	0781	0731	0747	07351	–	0746	0741	071
Sweden	00943	00932	0091	00945	009358	00933	00949	00944	00930	009353	00939	00981	00931	00947	009351	00934	–	00941	0091
Switzerland	0043	0032	001	0045	00358	0033	0049	0044	0030	00353	0039	0081	0031	0047	00351	0034	0046	–	001
USA	01143	01132	–	01145	011358	01133	01149	01144	01130	011353	01139	01181	01131	01147	011351	01134	01146	01141	–

If your exchange is not equipped to dial direct internationally, dial "0" and give the operator the number.

12 NOON — DUBLIN, LISBON, LONDON

1 PM — AMSTERDAM, MILAN, BRUSSELS, MUNICH, COPENHAGEN, OSLO, DUSSELDORF, PARIS, FRANKFURT, ROME, HAMBURG, STOCKHOLM, MADRID, VIENNA

2 PM — ATHENS, HELSINKI

8 PM — HONG KONG

9 PM — TOKYO

2 AM — ANCHORAGE, HONOLULU

4 AM — LOS ANGELES, SAN FRANCISCO, SEATTLE, VANCOUVER

5 AM — DENVER

6 AM — CHICAGO, KANSAS CITY, DALLAS, MEXICO CITY, DETROIT, NASHVILLE, HOUSTON, NEW ORLEANS, ST. LOUIS

7 AM — ATLANTA, NEW YORK, BOSTON, PHILADELPHIA, MIAMI, TORONTO, MONTREAL, WASHINGTON D.C.

9 AM — BUENOS AIRES

★ ★ ★ ★

COMPANY	AFFILIATE/LOCATION	PHONE #

ALLSTOCK
222 Dexter Ave N
Seattle, WA 98109
(800) 248-8116/(206) 622-6262

	ZEFA *Dusseldorf*	(49)(211) 5506-0 or
		(49)(211) 5506-1
	Pacific Press *Tokyo*	(81)(3) 3264-3821

AMERICAN STOCK PHOTOGRAPHY
6255 Sunset Blvd, Ste 716
Hollywood, CA 90028
(213) 469-3900

	Camerique Inc Int'l *Blue Bell*	(800) 272-4749 or
		(215) 272-4000
	Lewis, Frederic Stock Photos *NYC*	(800) 688-5656
	Orion Press *Tokyo*	(81)(3) 3295-1400

B.S.I.P.
34, Rue Villiers De L'Isle-Adam
F-75020 Paris, France
(33)(1) 43 58 69 87

	Custom Medical Stock Photo Inc *Chicago*	(800) 373-2677 or
		(302) 248-3200
	Science Photo Library *London*	(44)(71) 727-4712
	Stock Photos *Madrid*	(34)(1) 564-4095
	Marka S.R.L. *Milan*	(39)(2) 439-1628
	Superbild Archiv *Munich*	(49)(89) 6 41 77 77
	GU Press *Oslo*	(47)(2) 55 30 20
	International News Service *Tokyo*	(81)(3) 3571 0245

CAMERA TOKYO SERVICES CO LTD
6F Park Heights
Jignumae Shibuya-ku, Tokyo
(81)(3) 3407-7181

	Art Bank *Fukuoka*	(81)(92) 714-3274
	Sapporo Photo Live *Sapporo*	(81)(11) 222-1779
	Live Co Ltd *Sendai*	(81)(22) 224-1761
	Photo Bank Co *Taipei*	(886)(2) 506-3220

CAMERIQUE INC INT'L
1701 Skippack Pike
Blue Bell, PA 19422
(800) 272-4749/(215) 272-4000

	Jones, E.P. Co *Boston*	(617) 267-6450
	H. Armstrong Roberts *Chicago*	(312) 938-4466
	Stock Options *Dallas*	(214) 826-6262
	American Stock Photography *Hollywood*	(213) 469-3900
	H. Armstrong Roberts *NYC*	(212) 685-3870
	Lewis, Frederic Stock Photos *NYC*	(800) 688-5656
	Camerique/Florida *Sarasota*	(813) 351-5554
	Orion Press *Tokyo*	(81)(3) 3295-1400

COMSTOCK
30 Irving Pl
NYC, NY 10003
(212) 353-8600

	Comstock Fotoagentur *Berlin*	(49)(30) 462 90 90
	Comstock Agence Photographique *Boulogne*	(33)(1) 46 99 07 77
	Griggs, Susan Agency *London*	(44)(71) 385 8112
	Pacific Press *Tokyo*	(81)(3) 3264 3821
	Miller Comstock *Toronto*	(416) 925-4323

CONTACT PRESS IMAGES INC
116 E 27th St
NYC, NY 10016
(212) 481-6910

	Contrast Photo Agency *Athens*	(30)(1) 7230-236
	Focus Photo Und Pressagentur *Hamburg*	(49)(40) 443-769
	Colorific Photo Library *London*	(44)(71) 723-5031
	Cover *Madrid*	(34)(1) 327-2418
	Grazia Neri, SRL *Milan*	(39)(2) 805-3056
	Contact Press Images-Europe *Paris*	(33)(14) 357 4000
	Cosmos *Paris*	(33)(14) 705-4429
	Imperial Press *Tokyo*	(81)(3) 3585 2721

SEE PAGE 256 FOR DIALING INTERNATIONAL

★ ★ ★ ★

COMPANY	AFFILIATE/LOCATION	PHONE #

CUSTOM MEDICAL STOCK
3819 N Southport Ave
Chicago, IL 60613
(800) 373-2677/(312) 248-3200

Joel Science Photo Library *Amsterdam*	(31)(20) 20-420224
National Medical Slide Bank *Essex*	(44)(245) 283351
Fotex Medien Agentur GMBH *Hamburg*	(49)(40) 431-563
Science Photo Library *London*	(44)(71) 727-4712
Stock Photos *Madrid*	(34)(1) 564-4095
Marka S.R.L. *Milan*	(39)(2) 439-1628
B.S.I.P. *Paris*	(33)(1) 43 58 69 87
Auschromes Stock Agency *S Melbourne*	(61)(3) 699-3222

FPG INT'L
32 Union Square E
NYC, NY 10003
(212) 777-4210

FPG Int'l	*Over 30 agencies in 32 countries*

IMAGE BANK, THE
111 Fifth Ave
NYC, NY 10003
(212) 529-6700

The Image Bank Benelux *Amsterdam*	(31)(20) 679-19-91
The Image Bank Greece *Athens*	(30)(1) 867-5386
The Image Bank South *Atlanta*	(404) 233-9920
The Image Bank Thailand *Bangkok*	(66)(2) 237-6661
The Image Bank España *Barcelona*	(34)(3) 209-3544
The Image Bank Colombia *Bogota*	(57)(1) 610-8020
The Image Bank Boston *Boston*	(617) 267-8866
The Image Bank Benelux *Brussels*	(32)(2) 735-6762
The Image Bank Argentina *Buenos Aires*	(54)(1) 334-8121
The Image Bank South Africa *Capetown*	(27)(21) 24-4830
The Image Bank Venezuela *Caracas*	(58)(2) 959-2210
The Image Bank Hong Kong *Causeway Bay*	(852)(21) 576-2022
The Image Bank Chicago *Chicago*	(312) 329-1817
The Image Bank Denmark *Copenhagen*	(45) 33-15-15-24
The Image Bank Korea *Daegu*	(82)(53) 255-6356
The Image Bank Texas *Dallas*	(214) 528-3888
The Image Bank Germany *Frankfurt*	(49)(69) 430-171
The Image Bank Switzerland *Geneva*	(41)(22) 735-8511
The Image Bank Germany *Hamburg*	(49)(40) 280-1228
The Image Bank Finland *Helsinki*	(358)(0) 17-40-66
The Image Bank Texas *Houston*	(713) 668-0066
The Image Bank Turkey *Istanbul*	(90)(1) 157-0327
The Image Bank Indonesia *Jakarta*	(6621) 548-5746
The Image Bank Malaysia *Kuala Lumpur*	(60)(3) 254-7118
The Image Bank West *L.A.*	(213) 930-0797
The Image Bank Portugal *Lisbon*	(351)(1) 347-4707
The Image Bank *London*	(44)(71) 240-9621
The Image Bank France *Lyon*	(33)(7) 863-6950
The Image Bank España *Madrid*	(34)(1) 446-9061
The Image Bank *Manchester*	(44)(61) 236-9226
The Image Bank Australia *Melbourne*	(61)(3) 699-7833
The Image Bank Mexico *Mexico, D.F.*	(52)(5) 524-4644
The Image Bank Italia *Milan*	(39)(2) 86-93-964
The Image Bank Minneapolis *Minneapolis*	(612) 332-8935
The Image Bank Italia *Modena*	(39)(59) 920-263
The Image Bank Germany *Munich*	(49)(89) 418-69-30
The Image Bank South *Naples*	(813) 566-3444
The Image Bank Japan *Osaka*	(81)(6) 243-0300
The Image Bank Norway *Oslo*	(47)(2) 33-06-50
The Image Bank France *Paris*	(33)(14) 5-08-86-98
The Image Bank Brasil *Porto Alegre, RS*	(55)(512) 43-30-23

CONTINUED ON NEXT PAGE

COMPANY	AFFILIATE/LOCATION	PHONE #

IMAGE BANK, THE
111 Fifth Ave
NYC, NY 10003
(212) 529-6700

*CONTINUED FROM
PREVIOUS PAGE*

	AFFILIATE/LOCATION	PHONE #
	The Image Bank Chile *Providencia-Santiago*	(56)(2) 251-8473
	The Image Bank Brasil *Rio de Janeiro, RJ*	(55)(21) 267-1643
	The Image Bank Italia *Rome*	(39)(06) 482-4904
	The Image Bank West *S.F.*	(415) 788-2208
	The Image Bank Greece *Salonika*	(30)(31) 279-092
	The Image Bank South Africa *Sandton*	(27)(11) 883-7825
	The Image Bank Brasil *Sao Paulo, SP*	(55)(11) 852-3466
	The Image Bank Northwest *Seattle*	(206) 343-9319
	The Image Bank Korea *Seoul*	(82)(2) 273-27-92
	The Image Bank *Singapore*	(65) 338-3052
	The Image Bank Sweden *Stockholm*	(46)(8) 10-17-70
	The Image Bank Australia *Sydney*	(61)(2) 954-4255
	The Image Bank Taiwan *Taichung*	(886)(4) 227-4113
	The Image Bank Taiwan *Taipei*	(886)(2) 765-7364
	The Image Bank Israel *Tel-Aviv*	(972)(3) 510-4382
	The Image Bank Japan *Tokyo*	(81)(3) 3435-8360
	The Image Bank Canada *Toronto*	(416) 322-8840
	The Image Bank Detroit *Troy*	(313) 524-1850
	The Image Bank Austria *Vienna*	(43)(222) 505-3724
	The Image Bank Switzerland *Zurich*	(41)(1) 262-11-60

KIMBALL, RON STOCK
1960 Colony St.
Mountain View, CA 94043
(415) 969-0682

	Advertising Animals *Mountain View*	(415) 969-0682
	Advertising Automobiles *Mountain View*	(415) 969-0682

KRAMER, JOAN & ASSOCS INC
10490 Wilshire Blvd 605
LA, CA 90024
(310) 446-1866

	Joan Kramer & Assocs Inc *Great Neck*	(516) 466-5582
	Marka S.R.L. *Milan*	(39)(2) 72000155
	Kramer Joan, & Assocs Inc *NYC*	(212) 567-5545

LIFE PICTURE SALES
Time & Life Bldg
Rockefeller Ctr
NYC, NY 10020
(212) 522-4800

	ABC Press *Amsterdam*	(31)(20) 249413
	Roca-Sastre Agencia de Premsa, ACI *Barcelona*	(34)(3) 4872682
	IFOT APS *Copenhagen*	(45) 3138 6111
	Suomen Kuvapalvelu *Helsinki*	(358)(0) 156661555
	Katz Pictures *London*	(44)(71) 831 3370
	Grazia Neri *Milan*	(39)(2) 650 832 or (39)(2) 650 381
	Cosmos *Paris*	(33)(14) 705 4429
	Pacific Press Service	(81)(3) 3264 38214

MACH 2 STOCK EXCHANGE LTD, THE
1409 Edmonton Trl NE Ste 200
Calgary, Alberta T2E 3K8
(403) 230-9363

	Third Coast Stock Source *Milwaukee*	(414) 765-9442
	Hot Shots Stock Shots Inc *Toronto*	(416) 441-3281

PACIFIC STOCK PHOTOGRAPHY
3032 Holei St
Honolulu, HI 96815
(800) 321-3239/(808) 922-0975

	ZEFA *Dusseldorf*	(49)(211) 5506-0 or (49)(211) 5506-1
	Orion Press *Tokyo*	(81)(3) 3295 1440

SEE PAGE 256 FOR DIALING INTERNATIONAL

COMPANY	AFFILIATE/LOCATION	PHONE #
PANORAMIC IMAGES 230 N Michigan Ave Chicago, IL 60601 (800) 543-5250/(312) 236-8545	Photothèque Mon-Trésor Co Ltd *Osaka*	(81)(6) 344-3040
PEOPLE PHOTO & TEXT SYNDICATION Rockefeller Ctr Time & Life Bldg (212) 522-2453	**ABC Press** *Amsterdam* **Roca-Sastre Agency** *Barcelona* **IFOT APS** *Copenhagen* **Grazia Neri Agency** *Milan* **Imperial Press** *Tokyo*	(31)(20) 624 9413 (34)(3) 487 2662 (45) 3138 6111 (39)(2) 657 5172 (81)(3) 3585 2721
PHOTO EDIT 6056 Corbin Ave Tarzana, CA 91356 (818) 342-2811	**Olympia** *Milan*	(39)(2) 26 14 22 22
PICTURE CUBE, THE INC 89 Broad St Boston, MA 02210 (617) 367-1532	**Orion Press** *Tokyo*	(81)(3) 3295-1400
SHARPSHOOTERS 4950 SW 72nd Ave 114 Miami, FL 33155 (800) 666-1266/(305) 666-1266	**ZEFA Nederland B.V.** *Amsterdam* **ZEFA** *Dusseldorf* **ZEFA** *Frankfurt* **ZEFA** *Hamburg* **ZEFA Picture Library UK** *London* **ZEFA France S.A.R.L.** *Lyon* **ZEFA Italiana S.R.L.** *Milan* **ZEFA France S.A.R.L.** *Paris* **Auschromes Pty Ltd** *S Melbourne* **Sjoberg Press Service** *Stockholm* **Imperial Press** *Tokyo* **ZEFA** *Vienna* **ZEFA Farbbildagentur AG** *Zurich*	(31)(20) 66 138 66 (49)(211) 5506-0 or (49)(211) 5506-1 (49)(69) 75 80 4575 (49)(40) 4 10 20 83 (44)(71) 262-0101/5 (33)(7) 78 92 87 66 (39)(2) 48 00 45 25 (33)(14) 274-5547 (61)(3) 699-3222 (46)(8) 999 263 (81)(3) 585 2721 (43)(222) 32 74 50 (41)(1) 3 63 06 07
SPORTS CHROME EAST/WEST Ten Brinkerhoff Ave Palisades Park, NJ 07650 (201) 568-1412	**Sports Chrome West** *Walnut Creek*	(415) 398-7148
SPORTS ILLUSTRATED PICTURE SALES 1271 Ave of the Americas 20th fl NYC, NY 10020 (212) 522-4781	**Agencia de Premsa, ACI** *Barcelona* **Presse-Sports** *Cedex* **Colorific Photo Library** *London* **Grazia Neri** *Milan* **Pacific Press Service** *Tokyo*	(34)(1) 215 72 62 (33)(14) 4093-2032 (44)(71) 073-5031 (39)(2) 657 5172 (81)(33) 3264-3821

COMPANY	**AFFILIATE/LOCATION**	**PHONE #**

STARLIGHT PHOTO AGENCY
179 North Side Dr
Sag Harbor, NY 11963
(516) 725-5100

ABC Press Service *Amsterdam*	(31)(20) 249413
A.G.E FotoStock *Barcelona*	(34)(3) 300-2552
IFOT *Copenhagen*	(45)3138-6111
Focus *Hamburg*	(49)(40) 44 3769
Science Photo Library *London*	(44)(71) 727-4712
Grazia Neri *Milan*	(39)(2) 657-5172
Cosmos *Paris*	(33)(14) 705-4429
Pacific Press *Tokyo*	(81)(3) 3264 3821

STOCK MARKET, THE
360 Park Ave S 16th fl
NYC, NY 10010
(800) 999-0800/(212) 684-7878

ZEFA *Amsterdam*	(31)(20) 661 38 66
Benelux Press *Brussels*	(32)(2) 735-0772
IFOT *Copenhagen*	(45)3138-6111
ZEFA *Dusseldorf*	(49)(211) 5506-0 or
	(49)(211) 5506-1
ZEFA *Frankfurt*	(49)(69) 75 80 4575
ZEFA *Hamburg*	(49)(40) 4102083
Finnish Press Agency *Helsinki*	(358)(0) 15661
Stock House, The *Hong Kong*	(852) 886-0887
ZEFA *Leipzig*	(37)(41) 29 58 94
Agencia Dias Da Silva *Lisbon*	(351)(1) 823217
ZEFA Picture Library UK *London*	(44)(71) 262-0101/5
ZEFA France S.A.R.L. *Lyon*	(33)(7) 8 92 87 66
Stock Photos *Melbourne*	(61)(3) 699-7600
Granata Press Service *Milan*	(39)(2) 26680702
Kundsen *Oslo*	(47)(2) 422831
ZEFA France S.A.R.L. *Paris*	(33)(14) 274-5547
SIE *Rome*	(39)(6) 3241681
Sjoberg Press Service *Stockholm*	(46)(8) 999 263
Stock Photos *Sydney*	(61)(2) 954-3988
Visual Photo Library *Tel-Aviv*	(972)(3) 546-3433
Imperial Press *Tokyo*	(81)(3) 3585 2721
Masterfile *Toronto*	(416) 977-7267
ZEFA *Vienna*	(43)(222) 327450
ZEFA *Zurich*	(41)(1) 363 06 07

SUPERSTOCK
11 W 19th St
NYC, NY 10011
(800) 828-4545/(212) 633-0708

Segments Picture Library *Adelaide*	(61)(8) 231-4973
FotoStock *Amsterdam*	(31)(20) 664-2486
SuperStock Hellas *Athens*	(30)(1) 923-1651
Photobank Image Library *Auckland*	(64)(9) 773-178
A.G.E. FotoStock *Barcelona*	(34)(3) 300-2552
Firo-Foto *Barcelona*	(34)(3) 211-2593
Positive Image *Brisbane*	(617) 252-2894
Benelux Press *Brussels*	(32)(2) 735-0772
Bildagentur Mauritius *Brussels*	(32)(2) 762-9640
FourByFive Argentina *Buenos Aires*	(54)(1) 393-2265
Slide File, The *Dublin*	(353)(1) 686-086
Bavaria-Verlag Bildagentur *Dusseldorf*	(89)(211) 556-1080
Bildagentur Mauritius *Frankfurt*	(49)(69) 49-06-32
Key Photos *Fukuoka*	(81)(92) 781-8876
Lehtikuva Oy *Helsinki*	(358)(0) 122-4900
Stock House, The *Hong Kong*	(852)(5) 866-0887
SuperStock, S Africa *Johannesburg*	(27)(11) 788-8742

CONTINUED ON
NEXT PAGE

SEE PAGE 256 FOR DIALING INTERNATIONAL

COMPANY	AFFILIATE/LOCATION	PHONE #
SUPERSTOCK 11 W 19th St NYC, NY 10011 (800) 828-4545/(212) 633-0708 *CONTINUED FROM* *PREVIOUS PAGE*	**Bridgeman Art Library** *London*	(44)(71) 727-4065
	ZEFA Picture Library UK *London*	(44)(71) 262-0101/5
	ZEFA *Lyon*	(33)(7) 8 92 87 66
	SuperStock Australia *Melbourne*	(61)(3) 521-1716
	Franca Speranza S.R.L. *Milan*	(39)(2) 742-3297
	ZEFA Italiana S.R.L. *Milan*	(39)(2) 48-00-4525
	Bildagentur Mauritius *Mittenwald*	(49)(8) 823-5074
	SuperStock, Inc *Montreal*	(514) 849-2181
	Bavaria-Verlag Bildagentur *Munich*	(49)(89) 850-8044
	SuperStock Australia *N Sydney*	(61)(2) 920-5808
	Key Photos *Nagoya*	(81)(52) 261-2289
	Key Photos *Osaka*	(81)(6) 365-5620
	Orion Press *Osaka*	(81)(6) 252-5900
	Norsk Telegrambyra *Oslo 1*	(47)(2) 220-1670
	Agence VLOO *Paris*	(33)(14) 222-7016
	ZEFA *Paris*	(33)(14) 274-5547
	Key Stone *Rio de Janiero*	(55)(21) 253-9033
	SuperStock, Inc *S.F.*	(415) 781-4433
	Kactus Foto *Santiago*	(56)(2) 233-9884
	Key Stone *Sao Paulo*	(55)(11) 284-0173
	Key Photos *Seoul*	(82)(2) 272-2381
	Magnum Eye Co Inc *Seoul*	(82)(2) 275-8083
	APA Photos *Singapore*	(65) 737-2525
	Great Shots *Stockholm*	(46)(8) 107-260
	Bildagentur Mauritius *Stuttgart*	(49)(711) 226-23-99
	Key Photos *Taipei*	(886)(2) 597-7831
	Photo Bank Corp *Taipei*	(886)(2) 571-2071
	Visual Photo Library *Tel-Aviv*	(972)(3) 546-3433
	Key Photos *Tokyo*	(81)(3) 3409-4394
	Orion Press *Tokyo*	(81)(3) 3295-1400
	SuperStock, Inc *Toronto*	(416) 860-1518
	Bildagentur Mauritius *Vienna*	(43)(222) 82-31-840
	Benelux Press *Voorburg*	(31)(70) 387-1072
	Photo Index Researchers *W Perth*	(619) 481-0375
	Incolor Bildagentur *Zurich*	(41)(1) 361-7202
THIRD COAST STOCK SOURCE PO Box 92397 Milwaukee, WI 53202 (800) 323-9337/(414) 765-9442	**Mach 2 Stock Exchange Ltd, The** *Calgary*	(403) 230-9363
	Len Sirman Photos *Geneva*	(41)(22) 467128
	Fotex Medien Agentur GMBH *Hamburg*	(49)(40) 431-563
	Finnish Press Agency *Helsinki*	(358)(0) 15661
	Ace Photo Agency *London*	(44)(71) 629-0303
	Stock Photos *Madrid*	(34)(1) 564-4095
	Marka Graphic Photos & Archivium *Milan*	(39)(2) 72000155
	Reportagebild *Stockholm*	(46)(8) 725-25-00
	Mega Press Agency Inc *Tokyo*	(81)(3) 5485-2097
TIME PICTURE SYNDICATION Time & Life Bldg, Rockfeller Ctr 20th fl NYC, NY 10020 (212) 522-3593	**M. Issaris Press** *Athens*	(30)(1) 72 30 226
	Roca Sastre Agencia de Premsa, ACI *Barcelona*	(34)(3) 487 26 62
	Lehtikuva Oy Picture Agency *Helsinki*	(358)(0) 122 4909
	Katz Pictures Ltd *London*	(44)(71) 831 3370
	Masi Agency *Milan*	(39)(2) 952 3492
	Uniphoto Press Int'l Inc *Tokyo*	(81)(3) 3239 7002

★ ★ ★ ★

COMPANY	**AFFILIATE/LOCATION**	**PHONE #**

VERKERKE COPYRIGHT & LICENSING GMBH
CH-6403 Am Rigi Kuessnachf SZ
Im Fann, Switzerland
(41)(41) 81 50 38

Gallery Edition *NYC* (212) 862-4095

. . . .

VISUAL IMAGES WEST
600 E Baseline B6
Tempe, AZ 85283
(800) 433-4765/(602) 820-5403

Take Stock Photo Inc *Calgary*	(403) 233-7487
Fotex Medien Agentur GMBH *Hamburg*	(49)(40) 43-15-63
ACE Photo Agency *London*	(44)(71) 629-0303
Stock Photos *Madrid*	(34)(1) 564-4095
Marka S.R.L. *Milan*	(39)(2) 720-00155
Stock Image *Paris*	(33)(1) 48 04 00 09
Auschrome Pty Ltd *S Melbourne*	(61)(3) 699-3222
Megapress Agency Inc *Tokyo*	(81)(3) 5485-2097

. . . .

WILDLIFE COLLECTION, THE
69 Cranberry St
Brooklyn Heights, NY 11201
(800) 373-5151/(718) 935-9600

| Granata Press Service *Milan* | (39)(2) 26680702 |
| Orion Press *Tokyo* | (81)(3) 295 4006 |

SEE PAGE 256 FOR DIALING INTERNATIONAL

★ ★ ★ ★

LISTINGS

11th Hour, The/1313 W Randolph St, Chicago . . . . (312) 226-2661
29 Point 5/3712 Garfield Ave S, Mpls . . . . (612) 825-2900
A-Stock Photo Finder/230 N Michigan, Chicago . . . . (312) 645-0611
Adstock Photo/6219 N Ninth Pl, Phoenix . . . . (602) 277-5903
Adventure Photo/56 E Main St, Ventura . . . . (805) 643-7751
Advertising Animals/Mountain View/(415) 969-0682 . . . . **pages 22-23**
Advertising Automobiles/Mountain View/(415) 969-0682 . . . . **pages 20-21**
After Image/6100 Wilshire Blvd, L.A. . . . . (213) 938-1700
Ainsworth, Helen/5797 Scarborough Dr, Oakland . . . . (510) 531-7979
Alaska Pictorial Service/Anchorage . . . . (907) 344-1370
AlaskaStock Images/Anchorage/(800) 487-4285, (907) 276-1343 . . . . **pages 100-102**
Allen, J C & Son/1341 Northwestern Ave, W Lafayette . . . . (317) 463-9614
Allen, John E Inc/116 North Ave, Park Ridge . . . . (201) 391-3299
Allsport Photography/320 Wilshire Blvd, Santa Monica . . . . (310) 395-2955
AllStock/Seattle/(800) 248-8116, (206) 622-6262 . . . . **pages 199-233**
American Stock Photography/Hollywood/(213) 469-3900 . . . . **page 164**
Anatomy Works Inc/232 Madison Ave, NYC . . . . (212) 679-8480
Animals Animals/Earth Scenes/17 Railroad Ave, Chatham . . . . (518) 392-5500
Animals Animals/Earth Scenes/580 Broadway, NYC . . . . (212) 925-2110
Animals Animals/Earth Scenes/65 Bleecker St, NYC . . . . (212) 982-4442
Animates Ltd/1225 W Fourth St, Waterloo . . . . (319) 234-7055
Anthro-Photo File/33 Hurlbut St, Cambridge . . . . (617) 497-7227
Archive Photos/NYC/(800) 536-8445, (212) 675-0015 . . . . **pages 120-121**
Arnold, Peter Inc/NYC/(800) 289-7468, (212) 481-1190 . . . . **pages 107-116**
Art Resource/65 Bleecker St, NYC . . . . (212) 505-8100
Art Street/166 E Superior St, Chicago . . . . (312) 664-3561
Ashe, Bob/Denver . . . . (303) 592-1091
ASP Publishing/68 E Wacker, Chicago . . . . (312) 645-0611
Aspen Photo & Film Agency/1225 Alta Vista Dr, Aspen . . . . (303) 925-8280
Authenticated News Int'l/34 High St, Katonah . . . . (914) 232-7726
Baron Photography/Cleveland . . . . (216) 781-7729
Barth, Stephen Photography/37 S Clinton St, Doylestown . . . . (215) 340-0900
Beery, Gail/150 W Byers Pl, Denver . . . . (303) 777-0458
Berg & Assocs/6065 Mission Gorge Rd, San Diego . . . . (619) 284-8456
Bettmann/902 Broadway, NYC . . . . (212) 777-6200
Bilow, Nathan/Denver . . . . (303) 592-1091
Bishop, David/Food/251 W 19th St, NYC . . . . (212) 929-4355
Black Star/116 E 27th St, NYC . . . . (212) 679-3288
Blue Thunder Pictures/NYC/(212) 496-0908 . . . . **pages 148-149**
Brady, Steve/320 E 46th St, NYC . . . . (212) 941-6093
Brady, Steve/Houston . . . . (713) 660-6663
Brandt, Peter/73 Fifth Ave., NYC . . . . (212) 242-4289
Brooks & Assocs/855 W Blackhawk St, Chicago . . . . (312) 642-3208
Brown Brothers/100 Bortree Rd, Sterling . . . . (717) 689-9688
Buckley, Dana/Kids/136 Waverly Pl, NYC . . . . (212) 206-1807
Buzzelli, Rich/Denver . . . . (303) 592-1091
Camera 5/Six W 20th St, NYC . . . . (212) 989-2004
Camera Hawaii Inc/875 Waimanu St, Honolulu . . . . (808) 536-2302
Cameramann Int'l Ltd/Park Ridge . . . . (708) 825-4141
Camerique Inc Int'l/Blue Bell/(800) 272-4749, (215) 272-4000 . . . . **pages 145,164**
Camerique Stock Photography/3102 N Habana Ave, Tampa . . . . (813) 876-1868
CapeScapes/542 Higgens Cromwell Rd, W Yarmouth . . . . (508) 362-8222
Carstens & Amaral/3261 Ivanhoe, St. Louis . . . . (314) 647-0500
Cerulli, Nicholas/16 E 98th St, NYC . . . . (212) 563-3177
Charlton Photos Inc/11518 N Port Washington Rd, Mequon . . . . (414) 241-8634
Check Six/Tiburon/(415) 381-6363 . . . . **pages 26-29**
Chromosohm Media/11693 San Vicente Blvd, L.A. . . . . (310) 471-1915
Clifton, Carr/Taylorsville/(916) 284-6205 . . . . **pages 152-153**
Cohen, Stewart Charles/2401 S Ervay, Dallas . . . . (214) 421-2186
Collectors Series/7350 Croame Rd, Niles . . . . (708) 647-2211
Comstock/NYC/(800) 225-2727, (212) 353-8600 . . . . **pages 43-75**
Contact Press Images Inc/NYC/(212) 481-6910 . . . . **pages 192-193**

Coonrad, Jordan/1528A Lafayette St, Alameda . . . . (510) 769-9766
Cowgirl Stock Photography/1526 N Halsted, Chicago . . . . (312) 787-2778
Creative Photography/1927 Lee Blvd, N Mankado . . . . (507) 345-4208
Culver Pictures Inc/NYC/(212) 645-1672 . . . . **pages 24-25**
Curtis Management Group/Indpls/(317) 633-2050 . . . . **page 86**
Custom Medical Stock Photo Inc/Chicago/(800) 373-2677, (312) 248-3200 . . . . **pages 122-125**
Cyr Color Photo Agency/73 Benedict St, Norwalk . . . . (203) 838-8230
Dawson, Robert/Denver . . . . (303) 592-1091
DDB Productions/Denver . . . . (303) 592-1091
de Wys, Leo Inc/NYC/(800) 284-3399, (212) 689-5580 . . . . **pages 10-18**
Dembinsky Photo Assocs/5157 Hickory Hollow Ln, Owosso . . . . (517) 725-6902
Design Conceptions/112 Fourth Ave, NYC . . . . (212) 254-1688
Devaney Stock Photos Inc/755 New York Ave, Huntington . . . . (516) 673-4477
Diaz, Rick/4884 SW 74th Ct, Miami . . . . (305) 264-9761
Dot Picture Agency/NYC . . . . (212) 769-0158
DPI Inc/19 W 21st St, NYC . . . . (212) 627-4060
Drake, Brian & Assocs Inc/1300 NW Northrup, Portland . . . . (503) 228-2035
DRK Photo/265 Verde Valley School Rd, Sedona . . . . (602) 284-9808
Duomo Photography Inc/NYC/(212) 243-1150 . . . . **pages 2-3**
Earth Images/682 Winslow Way E, Bainbridge Is . . . . (206) 842-7793
Eastern Photo Service/1170 Broadway, NYC . . . . (212) 689-5580
EKM-Nepenthe/El Rito . . . . (505) 984-9719
Envision/220 W 19th St, NYC . . . . (212) 243-0415
Esto Photographics/222 Valley Pl, Mamaroneck . . . . (914) 698-4060
F-Stock Photography/Ketchum . . . . (208) 726-1378
F/Stop Pictures Inc/283 Kirk Meadow Rd, Springfield . . . . (802) 885-5261
Fashions In Stock/23-68 Steinway St, Astoria . . . . (718) 721-1373
First Light Assoc Photography/78 Rusholme Rd, Toronto . . . . (416) 532-6108
Florida Image File Inc/526 11th Ave, St Petersburg . . . . (813) 894-8433
Florida Photo Inventory Inc/5515 S Orange Ave, Orlando . . . . (407) 850-9499
Focus On Sports Inc/NYC/(212) 661-6860 . . . . **pages 154-159**
Focus Stock Photo Inc/950 Yonge St, Toronto . . . . (416) 968-6619
Folio Inc/3417 M St NW, Wash DC . . . . (202) 965-2410
Fotoconcept/408 SE 11th Ct, Ft Lauderdale . . . . (305) 463-1912
Four by Five Photography Inc/512 King St E, Toronto . . . . (416) 860-1518
FPG Int'l/NYC/(212) 777-4210 . . . . **pages 78-79**
Franz, Robert/Denver . . . . (303) 592-1091
Frederic Lewis/530 W 25th St, NYC . . . . (212) 620-3955
Friend, David/Life Magazine, New York . . . . (212) 522-4800
Frozen Images Inc/400 First Ave N, Mpls . . . . (612) 339-3191
Fumi Color Engineers/337 Summer St, Boston . . . . (617) 338-5409
Fundamental Photographs/210 Forsyth St, NYC . . . . (212) 473-5770
Gallery Edition/NYC/(212) 862-4095 . . . . **page 8**
Galloway, Ewing/100 Merrick Rd, Rockville Ctr . . . . (212) 719-4720
Gamba, Mark/115 W 23rd St, NYC . . . . (212) 727-8313
Gartman, Marilyn Photo Agency/510 N Dearborn, Chicago . . . . (312) 661-1656
Globe Photos Inc/275 Seventh Ave, NYC . . . . (212) 689-1340
Gluth Foto Team/173 E Grand Ave, Fox Lake . . . . (800) 243-3686
Gnass, Jeff Photography Inc/Portland/(503) 629-2020 . . . . **page 42**
Golfoto/224 N Independence, Enid . . . . (800) 338-1656
Gottlieb, Dennis/137 W 25th St, NYC . . . . (212) 620-7050
Granger Collection, The/381 Park Ave S, NYC . . . . (212) 447-1789
Great American Stock/7566 Trade St, San Diego . . . . (619) 271-9131
Green Source, The/3645 Jeannine Dr, Colorado Spgs . . . . (719) 570-1000
Green Stock/501-134 Abbott St, Vancouver . . . . (604) 688-9818
Green, Mark/Houston . . . . (713) 523-6146
Gross, Richard/Denver . . . . (303) 592-1091
Hall, George/Tiburon/(415) 381-6363 . . . . **pages 26-29**
Hanover Direct Inc/1500 Harbor Blvd, Weehawken . . . . (201) 863-7300
Hathon, Elizabeth/NYC . . . . (212) 219-0685
Headhunters/2619 Lovegrove St, Baltimore . . . . (410) 338-1820
Hedrich-Blessing/11 W Illinois St, Chicago . . . . (312) 321-1151
Heilman, Grant Photography Inc/506 W Lincoln Ave, Lititz . . . . (800) 622-2046
Heuberger, William/140 W 22nd St, NYC . . . . (212) 242-1532
Hillstrom Stock Photo Inc/5483 N Northwest Hwy, Chicago . . . . (312) 775-4090
Historical Pictures Service/Chicago/(312) 733-3239 . . . . **page 4**

McCann Co, The/4113A Rollins St, Dallas	(214) 526-2252
McGraw, Ken/Denver	(303) 592-1091
McLoughlin, James/148 W 24th St, NYC	(212) 206-8207
Mead, Joyce/Palisades Pk/(201) 568-1412	**page 240**
Medical Images Inc/26 W Shore Pl, Salisbury	(203) 824-7858
Medical Link-Phototake Inc/NYC/(800) 542-3686, (212) 942-8185	**pages 162-163**
Meyerson, Arthur/4215 Bellaire Blvd, Houston	(713) 660-0405
Miller Comstock/Toronto/(800) 387-0640, (416) 925-4323	**pages 43-75**
Miller, Mark & Jennifer/Denver	(303) 592-1091
Minden Pictures/119A Marina Ave, Aptos	(408) 685-1911
Mon-Trésor/W-catalog/Chicago/(800) 543-5250, (312) 236-8545	**pages 236-237**
Mon-Trésor/Y-catalog/Chicago/(800) 356-3066, (312) 427-8625	**pages 38-39**
Morris, J L/Denver	(303) 592-1091
Motion Picture & TV Photo Archive/11821 Mississippi Ave, L.A.	(310) 478-2379
Mountain Stock Photography & Film Inc/Tahoe City/(916) 583-6646	**pages 30-31**
Muench, David/Santa Barbara	(805) 967-4488
MugShots/30 Rockledge Rd, W Redding	(203) 938-3246
Murray's J2/4136 Hillcrest Ave SW, Seattle	(206) 937-9235
National Stock Network/8960 SW 114th St, Miami	(305) 233-1703
Natural Selection Stock Photo Inc/Rochester/(716) 232-1502	**pages 146-147**
Nawrocki Stock Photo/Chicago/(800) 356-3066, (312) 427-8625	**pages 39-41,182**
NBA Photos/645 Fifth Ave, NYC	(212) 826-7000
Network Images/545 Hyde St, S.F.	(415) 771-5986
New England Stock Photography/18 Briar Cliff Trl, Old Saybrook	(203) 388-1741
New Image Stock Photography/38 Quail Ct, Walnut Creek	(510) 934-2405
Newsom, Carol/Framingham/(508) 877-8795	**page 178**
NFL Photos/L.A./(310) 215-1606	**pages 98-99**
Odyssey Productions/4158 N Greenview St, Chicago	(312) 883-1965
Omni-Photo Communications/Five E 22nd St, NYC	(212) 995-0805
Oudi Stock Photography/33 Bleecker St, NYC	(212) 777-0847
Pacific Stock Photography/Honolulu/(800) 321-3239, (808) 922-0975	**pages 118-119**
Page Assocs/219 E 69th St, NYC	(212) 772-0346
Panoramic Images/Chicago/(800) 543-5250, (312) 236-8545	**pages 236-237**
Pantages, Tom/34 Centre St, Concord	(603) 224-1489
Parsons, Jack/355 E Palace Ave, Santa Fe	(505) 984-8092
Peebles, Douglas Photography/445 Iliwahi Loop, Kailua	(808) 254-1082
People Photo & Text Syndication/NYC/(212) 522-2453	**pages 33,37**
Photo 20-20/50 Kenyon Ave, Kensington	(510) 526-0921
Photo Agents Ltd/113 E 31st St, NYC	(212) 683-5777
Photo Edit/Tarzana/(818) 342-2811	**pages 150-151**
Photo File, The/110 Pacific Ave, S.F.	(415) 397-3040
Photo Network/1541-J Parkway Loop, Tustin	(800) 548-0199
Photo Options/2206 Gill St, Huntsville	(205) 533-4331
Photo Researchers/60 E 56th St, NYC	(212) 758-3420
Photo Resource Hawaii/1146 Fort St, Honolulu	(808) 599-7773
Photo Resources/511 Broadway, Saratoga Spgs	(800) 627-4686
Photo Stock Unlimited/7208 Thomas Blvd, Pittsburgh	(215) 242-5070
Photobank Inc/17592-B Skypark Cir, Irvine	(714) 250-4480
Photobank, The/313 E Thomas Rd, Phoenix	(602) 265-5591
Photographers/Aspen/1280 Ute Ave, Aspen	(303) 925-2317
Photographic Assoc of Texas/Tomball	(713) 255-8476
Photographic Resources Inc/St Louis/(800) 933-5838, (314) 721-5838	**pages 82-83**
Photography for Industry/1697 Broadway, NYC	(212) 757-9255
Photonet/2655 Lejeune Road, Miami	(800) 875-3686
Photonica/141 Fifth Ave, NYC	(212) 366-1111
Photophile/2311 Kettner Blvd, San Diego	(619) 234-4431
Photoreporters Inc/875 Ave of the Americas, NYC	(212) 736-7602
Photosearch/Milwaukee	(414) 271-5777
Photosource Int'l/Pine Lake Farm, Osceola	(715) 248-3800
Phototake Inc-The Creative Link/NYC/(800) 542-3686, (212) 942-8185	**pages 162-163**
Photothèque Mon-Trésor/W-catalog/Chicago/(800) 543-5250, (312) 236-8545	**pages 236-237**
Photothèque Mon-Trésor/Y-catalog/Chicago/(800) 356-3066, (312) 427-8625	**pages 38-39**
Photovault/1045 17th St, S.F.	(415) 552-9682
Photri-Photo Research/3701 S George Mason Rd, Falls Church	(703) 931-8600
Pictorial History Research/565 Meadow Rd, Winnetka	(708) 446-5987
Pictorial Parade Inc/530 W 25th St, NYC	(212) 840-2026

Stone, Tony Worldwide/Chicago Ltd/233 E Ontario, Chicago .... (800) 234-7880
Stone, Tony Worldwide/L.A. Ltd/6100 Wilshire Blvd, L.A. .... (213) 938-1700
Streano Havens/Anacortes .... (206) 293-4525
SuperStock/NYC/(800) 828-4545, (212) 633-0300 .... pages 5,103,175,252
SuperStock/S.F./(800) 828-4545, (415) 781-4433 .... pages 5,103,175,252
Superstock Int'l Inc/Ten W 20th St, NYC .... (212) 633-0200
Take Stock Photography/405-603 Seventh Ave SW, Calgary .... (403) 233-7487
Team Russell/210 C Ventnor, Aspen .... (303) 920-1431
Telephoto/Eight Thomas St, NYC .... (212) 406-2440
Third Coast Stock Source/Milwaukee/(800) 323-9337, (414) 765-9442 .... pages 183-191
Thomas, Bob Sports Photography/Framingham/(508) 877-8795 .... page 178
Tigerhill Studio/4234 Howard, Western Springs .... (708) 246-3566
Time Picture Syndication/NYC/(212) 522-3593 .... pages 33-34
Tobias, Jerry/2117 Opa Locka Blvd, Miami................................. (305) 685-3003
Tom Tracy Photography/One Maritime Plz, S.F. .... (415) 340-9811
Travel Vues/Norman Ehrenberg/6342 Beeman Ave, N Hollywood .... (213) 877-1701
Underwood Photo Archives/S.F./(415) 346-2292 .... page 106
Uniphoto Picture Agency/3205 Grace St NW, Wash DC...................... (202) 333-0500
Vaughn, Marc/11140 Griffing Blvd, Biscayne Park .... (305) 895-5790
Vedros, Nick & Assocs/NYC .... (212) 473-3366
Vedros, Nick & Assocs/Chicago .... (312) 444-2052
Vedros, Nick & Assocs/215 W 19th St, Kansas City .... (816) 471-5488
Vermont Stock Photo/22 Crescent Beach Dr, Burlington .... (802) 862-5912
Viesti Assocs/627 West End Ave, NYC .... (212) 734-4890
View Finder/2310 Penn Ave, Pittsburgh .... (412) 391-8720
Viewfinders Inc/126 N Third St, Mpls .... (612) 333-8170
Viewing Room, The/39 S LaSalle, Chicago .... (312) 684-7500
Visions Photo Inc/220 W 19th St, NYC................................... (212) 255-4047
Visual File/1039 Seventh Ave, San Diego .... (619) 232-3366
Visual Images West Inc/Tempe/(800) 433-4765, (602) 820-5403 .... page 80
Visual Impact Hawaii/Honolulu/(808) 524-8269 .... page 19
Visual Media Inc/1877 Purdue Dr, Reno .... (702) 322-8868
Volcanic Resources/Volcano.. (808) 967-7672
Walker, Tom/Denver.. (303) 592-1091
Wark, Jim/Denver .... (303) 592-1091
Waterhouse Stock Photography/Key Largo/(800) 451-3737 .... pages 194-195
Weens, Clifford/15 Office Park Cir, Birmingham .... (205) 871-1066
Weinstein, David/1255 S Michigan Ave, Chicago........................... (312) 427-9600
West Light/2223 S Carmelina Ave, L.A. .... (800) 872-7872
West Stock/83 S King, Seattle .... (206) 621-1611
Wild Pic Int'l/1818 16th St, Boulder...................................... (303) 440-9453
Wildlife Collection, The/Brooklyn Heights/(800) 373-5151, (718) 935-9600 .... page 132
Wolf, Brian Photography/11505 Hitching Post Ln, Rockville .... (212) 465-8976
Zehrt, Jack/18920 Deer Creek Rd, Pacific .... (314) 458-3600
Zephyr Pictures/Del Mar/(800) 537-3794, (619) 755-1200 .... pages 196-197
Zooligical Society/2920 Zoo Dr, San Diego .... (619) 231-1515

I N T E R N A T I O N A L

SEE PAGE 256 FOR DIALING INTERNATIONAL GUIDE

3F Produkties/Frank Greiner/De Visserlaan 2, Uithoorn, Neth .... (31)(2975) 6 67 60
AA Photo Library/Fanum House, Hants, UK .... (44)(256) 493307
AAA Photo/44 Rue de Varenne, Paris, Fr .... (33)(1) 45 48 53 11
ABC Press Service/O.Z. Achterburgwal 141, Amsterdam, Neth .... (31)(20) 24 94 13
Abrahams, Kate/1a Roman Rd, London, UK .... (44)(71) 747 1082
ACE Photo Agency/22 Maddox St, London, UK............................ (44)(71) 629 5095
Adams Picture Library/156 New Cavendish St, London, UK .... (44)(71) 636 1468
Adlib Photo Agency/33 Albury Ave, Isleworth, Middx, UK.................. (44)(81) 847 3777
AFIP/2 Rue Paul Escudier, Paris, Fr .... (33)(1) 48 74 52 88
AFLO Photo Agency/Okatsu Boulevard, Chuo-ku Tokyo, Jp .... (81)(3) 546 0260
AFP/13 Place de la Bourse, Paris, Fr.................................... (33)(1) 40 41 46 46
AGE Fotostock/Buenaventura Munoz, Barcelona 08018, Sp .... (34)(3) 300 2552
Agence D'Illustration Pour La Press/32 Rue du Sentier, Paris, Fr .... (33)(1) 42 36 42 20
Agence de Presse Imapress/22 rue Guillaume-Tell, Paris, Fr .... (33)(1) 47 66 83 31

Agence Ernoult Features/8 Rue des Favorites, Paris, Fr . . . . (33)(1) 42 50 77 70
Agence Kid/9 Rue des Freres Greban, Le Mans Cedex, Fr . . . . (33)(43) 24 65 75
Agencia Dias Da Silva/Lisbon/(351)(1) 823217 . . . . page 144
Air Pictures/69 Ave de la Bour Donnais, Paris, Fr . . . . (33)(1) 45 55 52 58
Aird Associations/18 Upper Park Rd, London, UK . . . . (44)(71) 722 6548
All Sport France/61/63 Rue des Entre Preneups, Paris, Fr . . . . (33)(1) 45 79 88 54
All-Sport Ltd/Greenlea Park, London, UK . . . . (44)(71) 685 1010
AMPP/11 Rue GJ Martin, Bruxelles, Belg . . . . (32)(2) 762 96 40
ANA/6 Avenue Rene Coty, Paris, Fr . . . . (33)(1) 43 35 28 38
Ancient Art & Architecture Photo Lib/6 Kenton Rd, Harrow, UK . . . . (44)(81) 422 1214
Angeli/35 Rue Victor Hugo, Levallois-Perret, Fr . . . . (33)(47) 39 00 00
Animal Photography/4 Marylebone Mews, London, UK . . . . (44)(71) 935 0503
ANP Photo/Wibautstraat 129, Amsterdam, Neth . . . . (31)(20) 568 56 85
AP/162 Rue du Fbg St Honore, Paris, Fr . . . . (33)(1) 42 56 09 72
APA/3 Rue Constance, Paris, Fr . . . . (33)(1) 42 52 11 58
Aquila Photographics/Alcester Rd, Studley, UK . . . . (44)(527) 85 2357
Arcadia/23 Rue des Apennins, Paris, Fr . . . . (33)(1) 42 63 68 44
Arcaid/Surrey/(44)(81) 546 4352 . . . . page 1
ArchiPress/16 Rue Pierre Levee, Paris, Fr . . . . (33)(1) 43 38 51 81
Arctic Camera, Derek Fordham/66 Ashburnham Grove, London, UK . . . . (44)(81) 692 7651
Ardea London Ltd/35 Brodrick Rd, London, UK . . . . (44)(71) 672 2067
Arnault, Francoise/137 Vieille du Temple, Paris, Fr . . . . (33)(1) 42 74 34 94
Art Bank/Green Mansion 4-31 Imaizumi, Chuoku Fukuoka, Jp . . . . (81)(92) 714 3274
Art Directors Photo Library/London/(44)(71) 485 9325 . . . . page 117
Art Documentation System/Amstel 218, Amsterdam, Neth . . . . (31)(20) 24 18 53
Aspect Picture Library Ltd/40 Rostrevor Rd, London, UK . . . . (44)(71) 736 1998
Associated Press/Fluelastr 47, Zurich, Switz . . . . (44)(1) 491 96 33
Auschromes Pty Ltd/Melbourne/(61)(3)699 3222 . . . . pages 165-173
Australasian Nature Transparencies/22 Martin St, Victoria, Ausl . . . . (61)(3) 458 4588
Australian Picture Library/12-14 Falcon St, Sydney, Ausl . . . . (61)(2) 438 3011
Aviemore Photographic, Staney , Pavel./Main Rd, Aviemore, Scot . . . . (44)(479) 810371
B & U Int'l Picture Service/2e Jan van Heijdenstr 85, Amsterdam, Neth . . . . . (31)(20) 662 95 51
BAPLA/13 Woodberry Crescent, London, UK . . . . (44)(81) 883 2531
Barda, Clive/50 Agate Rd, London, UK . . . . (44)(81) 741 0805
Barnaby's Picture Library/19 Rathbone St, London, UK . . . . (44)(71) 636 6128
BBC Hulton Picture Library/35 Marylebone High St, London, UK . . . . (44)(71) 927 4735
BBC Picture Library/Cavendish Pl, London, UK . . . . (44)(71) 580 4468
Beeldbank en Uitgeefprojekten BV/Postbus 51245, Amsterdam, Neth . . . . . . (31)(20) 662 95 51
Beken of Cowes Ltd/16 Birmingham Rd, Isle of Wight, UK . . . . (44)(983) 297 311
Benelux Press BV/Brussels/(32)(2) 735 0772 . . . . page 144
Benelux Press BV/Voorburg, Neth . . . . (31)(70) 87 04 70 87
Bernand/106 Rue de Richelieu, Paris, Fr . . . . (33)(1) 42 97 41 73
Bernand Seigneury Conseil/43 Villiers, Paris, Fr . . . . (33)(1) 43 58 69 87
Bild + News AG B + N/Foto- und Presseagentur, Zurich, Switz . . . . (41)(1) 491 96 50
Bildagentur Baumann AG/Breitenstr 9, Wurenlingen/AG, Switz . . . . (41)(056) 98 1231
Bildagentur Mauritius/Kupelwiesergasse 16, Wien, Ger . . . . (43)(222) 82 31840
Bildagentur Mauritius/Baumweg 19, Frankfurt, Ger . . . . (49)(69) 49 06 32
Bildagentur Mauritius/Alpencorpsstr 15, Mittenwald, Ger . . . . (49)(8) 823 5074
Biofotos/6 Vicarage Hill, Farnham, Surrey, UK . . . . (44)(252) 716 700
Bios/23 Rue des Blancs Manteaux, Paris, Fr . . . . (33)(1) 40 29 90 69
Blake, Anthony/54 Hill Rise, Richmond, Surrey, UK . . . . (44)(81) 940 7583
Blue C Press/29 Bernhard Bangs Alle, Frederiksberg, Den . . . . (45)(1) 86 60 11
Blue Sky/33 Rue Godot Mauroy, Paris, Fr . . . . (33)(1) 42 65 86 81
BMV Picturebank/79 Farrington Rd, London, UK . . . . (44)(71) 405 5021
Bourgeois, Nicole/4 Rue Van Canson, Paris, Fr . . . . (33)(1) 42 77 68 73
Box Office/19 Rue Brey, Paris, Fr . . . . (33)(1) 46 22 89 90
Boys Syndication/Red House Newbourne, Suffolk, UK . . . . (44)(047) 336 333
Brecht-Einzig/6 Latchmere Rd, London, UK . . . . (44)(71) 546 4352
Bridgeman Art Library, The/19 Chepstow Rd, London, UK . . . . (44)(71) 727 4065
British Film Institute/127-133 Charing Cross Rd, London, UK . . . . (44)(71) 437 4355
British Tourist Authority/239 Old Marylebone Rd, London, UK . . . . (44)(71) 262 0141
BSIP/Paris/(33)(1) 43 58 69 87 . . . . pages 124-125
Bulloz/21 Rue Bonaparte, Paris, Fr . . . . (33)(1) 43 26 54 76
Camera Press/Russell Ct Coram St, London, UK . . . . (44)(71) 837 4488
Camera Tokyo Services Co Ltd/Tokyo/(81)(3) 3407 7181 . . . . pages 180-181
Campagne-Campagne/156 Rue du Fbg Poissoniere, Paris, Fr . . . . (33)(1) 42 85 79 80

Cartographisch Bureau van Pelt/Jan Luyken-Straat 28, Amsterdam, Neth . . . . (31)(20) 79 55 50
CEDRI/10 Rue The Rese, Paris, Fr . . . . (33)(1) 42 96 08 07
Chamarat, Jocelyne/116 Rue St-Dominique, Paris, Fr . . . . (33)(1) 47 05 26 99
Chamid, Soenar/Berkelstraat 3, Almere-stad, Neth . . . . (31)(3240) 3 32 31
Cinemagence/12 Rue Saulnier, Paris, Fr . . . . (33)(1) 42 46 21 21
CIRIC/6 Rue Jean Lantier, Paris, Fr . . . . (33)(1) 42 33 92 94
CLAM/35 Rue Montpensier, Paris, Fr . . . . (33)(1) 42 96 84 84
Cloos Lionelle/62 Bd Richard Lendir, Paris, Fr . . . . (33)(1) 47 00 20 25
CNAP/113 Rue des Moines, Paris, Fr . . . . (33)(1) 42 28 89 89
CNRI/4 Ave Constant Coquelin, Paris, Fr . . . . (33)(1) 45 67 71 71
Colasanti, Stepanie-Travel Worldwide/38 Hillside Ct, London, UK . . . . (44)(71) 435 3695
Coleman, Bruce Ltd/17 Windsor St, Middlesex, UK . . . . (44)(895) 57094
Colin Gratt's/The Square Newton Harcourt, Leicestershire, UK . . . . (44)(53) 759 2068
Colorific! Le Goubin/Gloucester Ter, London, UK . . . . (44)(71) 723 5031
Colorsport/44 St Peter's St, London, UK . . . . (44)(71) 359 2714
Colotheque/Avenue Paul Hymanslaan 103, Bruxelles, Belg . . . . (32)(2) 762 48 07
Combi Press Service/Plantage Parklaan 12, Amsterdam, Neth . . . . (31)(20) 24 67 43
Comet-Photo AG/Turnerstr 7a, Zurich, Switz . . . . (41)(1) 361 97 80
Comstock Agence Photographique/Boulogne/(33)(1) 46 99 07 77 . . . . **pages 43-75**
Comstock Fotoagentur/Berlin/(49)(30) 462 9090 . . . . **pages 43-75**
Contact Press Images Inc/Paris/(33)(1) 43 57 40 00 . . . . **pages 192-193**
Cosmopress Hassberger A & Cie/11 chemin Falletti, Genf/GE, Switz . . . . (41)(22) 49 32 33
Cosmos/56 Blvd de la Tour Maubourg, Paris, Fr . . . . (33)(1) 4705 44
Daily Telegraph Colour Library/99 Shone Ln, London, UK . . . . (44)(71) 353 4242
Das Photo, Cherry Trees/Queen's Rd, Bisley, Surrey, UK . . . . (44)(4867) 3395
Davis, James Travel Photog/30 Hengistbury Rd, New Milton Hants, UK . . . . (44)(4867) 3395
Deporte, Delphine/62 bis Rue Jean Jaures, Levallois-Perret, Fr . . . . (33)(42) 70 65 26
Derksen, Api E/Redingstr 20/16, Basel, Switz . . . . (41)(61) 312 32 46
Destremau, Dominique/7 Place deL'Estra Pade, Paris, Fr . . . . (33)(1) 46 33 37 64
Deue, Francoise/46 Rue de Turbigo, Paris, Fr . . . . (33)(1) 42 74 16 33
Devim Studio/Entrepotdok 61a, Amsterdam, Neth . . . . (31)(20) 22 45 75
DIAF S.a.r.l./30 Rue Vieille du Temple, Paris, Fr . . . . (33)(1) 42 71 69 96
Diaphor/La Phototheque/18 Parvis St Michel, Lille, Fr . . . . (33)(20) 54 17 78
DITE, Thierry Eteve/10 Rue de L'Isly, Paris, Fr . . . . (33)(1) 45 22 06 62
Domic Photography/9a Netherton Grv, London, UK . . . . (44)(71) 352 6118
DPPI/75 Rue Voltaire, Levallois-Perret, Fr . . . . (33)(47) 39 93 60
Du Jour, Nane/27 Rue du 19 Janvier, Garches, Fr . . . . (33)(47) 41 59 17
Du Moulin, Veronique/18 Rue Dugommier, Paris, Fr . . . . (33)(1) 43 41 32 64
Ducatez JPDB/56 Rue Caulaincourt, Paris, Fr . . . . (33)(1) 46 06 83 32
Dukas, Presse-Agentur, L/Witikonerstr 98, Zurich, Switz . . . . (41)(1) 53 96 30
Duncan, Ken/Wamberal, Ausl . . . . (61)(043) 67 6777
Dutch Slide Store/Pim Westerweel/Bollelaan 2, Bussum, Neth . . . . (31)(2159) 43108
Edimedia/58 Rue Beaubourg, Paris, Fr . . . . (33)(1) 48 87 73 73
Enguerand/CDDS/16 Rue du Fbg Montmartre, Paris, Fr . . . . (33)(1) 48 24 18 82
Eole Photo/JP Leloir/26 Rue Notre Dame des Victoire, Paris, Fr . . . . (33)(1) 42 96 27 97
Eskimo/12 Rue St Joseph, Paris, Fr . . . . (33)(1) 42 96 27 97
Evans, Mary Picture Library/59 Tranquil Vale, London, UK . . . . (44)(81) 314 0034
Explorer/60 Rue de Richelieu, Paris, Fr . . . . (33)(1) 42 96 85 50
Farbdia-Archiv, Edmond van Hoorick/Richterwil/ZH, Switz . . . . (41)(1) 784 42 72
Farbild-Archiv Siegfried Eigstler/Obere Wart 53d, Thun/BE, Switz . . . . (41)(033) 23 44 66
Finnish Press Agency/Helsinki/(358)(0) 15661 . . . . **page 144**
Fotex Medien Agentur GMBH/Glashutienstrasse 79, 2000 Hamburg 36, Ger . . . . . (49)(40) 431 563
Foto Stockbury plus Fotopersbu ro/Nico van der Stam, Amsterdam, Neth . . . . (31)(20) 79 17 92
Fotobank Int'l/30 Kingly Ct, London, UK . . . . (44)(71) 734 4764
FOTOGRAM-STONE/45 Rue de Richelieu, Paris, Fr . . . . (33)(1) 42 96 03 07
Fotostock BV/Argonautenstraat 17, Amsterdam, Neth . . . . (31)(20) 664 24 86
Fournier, Michele/84 Av Niel, Paris, Fr . . . . (33)(1) 47 66 37 64
FOVEA/3 Rue Leon Cogniet, Paris, Fr . . . . (33)(1) 42 27 33 96
Galaxy Contract/7 Rue Gustave Cuvelier, Calais Cedex, Fr . . . . (33)(21) 35 25 15
Garanger, Marc/76 bis Rue Vieille du Temple, Paris, Fr . . . . (33)(1) 42 77 90 85
Garden Picture Library, The/Unit 15, 35 Parkgate Rd, London, UK . . . . (44)(71) 228 4332
Gauvreau, Odile/108 Rue de la Convention, Paris, Fr . . . . (33)(1) 42 77 90 85
Gerster, Dr Georg/Tobelhusstr 24, Zumikon, Switz . . . . (41)(1) 918 10 25
Giraudon/92 Rue de Richelieu, Paris, Fr . . . . (33)(1) 42 96 10 44
Granata Press Service/Milan/(39)(2) 26680702 . . . . **page 144**
Grazia Neri/Via Parini 9, Milan, Ital . . . . (39)(2) 657 5172

Griffel, Josef/Neugasse 27, Baar/ZG, Switz . . . . (41)(42) 31 96 39
Hanekroot Gijsbert/Kromboomsloot 63, Amsterdam, Neth . . . . (31)(20) 20 14 40
Harding, Robert Picture Library/17a Newman St, London, UK . . . .(44)(71) 637 8969
Henstra, Taeke/Lange Lakenstraat 16-18, Haarlem, Neth . . . . (31)(23) 32 39 93
Hoa-Qui/145 Rue St Dominique, Paris, Fr . . . . (33)(1) 47 05 16 28
Hollandse Hoogte/Lindengracht 168 hs, Amsterdam, Neth . . . . (31)(20) 27 61 19
Horizon/144 Pacific Hwy, North Sydney, Ausl . . . . (61)(2) 957 5412
Horizon/7 Bury Place, London, UK . . . .(44)(71) 831 1109
IF Creation/Herve Nabon/6 Rue de L'Armee D'Orient, Paris, Fr . . . . (33)(1) 42 64 32 95
IFOT/Copenhagen/(45)(31)386111 . . . . **page 144**
Ilonos/4 Place Sathonay, Lyon, Fr . . . . (33)(7) 78 28 24 27
Image Bank/Strawinskylaan 1129, Amsterdam, Neth . . . . (31)(20) 575 33 24
Image Bank France, The/130 Rue Reaumur, Paris, Fr . . . . (33)(1) 45 08 86 98
Image Bank London, The/7 Langley St, London, UK . . . . (46)(71) 240 9621
Image Bank, The/Dufourstr 56/Postfach, Zurich, Switz . . . . (41)(1) 262 11 60
Imapress/22 Rue Guillaume Tell, Paris, Fr . . . . (33)(1) 78 28 24 27
IMPACT Photos/26-27 Great Sutton St, London, UK . . . .(44)(71) 251 5091
Imperial Press/Tokyo/(81)(3) 3585 2721 . . . . **pages 144,165-173**
Incolor Ag Schweiz/Vogelsangstr 48, Zurich, Switz . . . . (41)(1) 361 72 02
Innofot/80 Rue Laugier, Paris, Fr . . . . (33)(1) 46 22 13 18
Inter-Topics/Billbrookdeich 36, Hamburg, Ger . . . . (49)(40) 732 03 71
International Photo Library/Don Sutton 11 Eglinton Ct, Dublin 4/Ire . . . .(353)(1) 696 684
International Picture Service/Amsterdam, Neth . . . . (31)(20) 662 95 51
Interpress/16 bis Rue Fontaine, Paris, Fr . . . . (33)(1) 42 81 20 20
Jacana/30 Rue St Marc, Paris, Fr . . . . (33)(1) 42 33 04 04
Jerrican/33 Rue Etienne-Marcel, Paris, Fr . . . . (33)(1) 42 33 04 04
Jet Set/26 Avenue George V, Paris, Fr . . . . (33)(1) 47 20 11 25
Jimagine Group/15 Rue de Strasbourg, Grenoble, Fr . . . . (33)(76) 54 28 40
Joel Science Photo Library/Strawinfklaan, 1077 Amsterdam, Neth . . . . (31)(20) 204 20224
Joel, A.J./Ernststraat 181, Amsterdam, Neth . . . . (31)(20) 42 02 73
Joly, Anne/5 Rue Antoine Vollon, Paris, Fr . . . . (33)(1) 43 46 88 79
Keel, Paul/Friesenbergstr 94, Zurich, Switz . . . . (41)(1) 462 78 41
Keller Topcom/Zweierstr 129, Zurich, Switz . . . . (41)(1) 461 55 33
Kerneis, Michele/42 Rue de Chabrol, Paris, Fr . . . . (33)(1) 48 24 57 76
Keycolor, Farbdia Agentur/Grubenstr 45, Zurich, Switz . . . . (41)(1) 462 06 20
Keystone Press AG/Grubenstr 45, Zurich, Switz . . . . (41)(1) 462 02 78
Keystone Press Agency/25 Rue Royale, Paris, Fr . . . . (33)(1) 42 65 64 02
Kipa/12 Rue Martel, Paris, Fr . . . . (33)(1) 47 70 64 13
Krief, Denise/222 Rue du Fbg St Denis, Paris, Fr . . . . (33)(1) 46 07 91 31
Kundsen/Oslo/(47)(2) 422831 . . . . **page 144**
Kuvasuomi/Vantaa, Fin . . . .(358)(0) 890 233
La Phototheque S-D-P/9 Turbigo, Paris, Fr . . . . (33)(1) 40 26 16 02
La Phototheque SGM/19 Av de la Liberte, Strasbourg-Cedex, Fr . . . . (33)(88) 35 45 26
Labhardt, Felix/Bruderholzstr 26, Bottmingen/BL, Switz . . . . (41)(61) 47 05 16
Laguens, Michel/47 Avenue Paul Doumer, Paris, Fr . . . . (33)(1) 45 03 37 53
Landscape Only/60 Poland St, London, UK . . . .(44)(71) 437 2655
Larsen, Anne/6 Quai des Celestins, Paris, Fr . . . . (33)(1) 42 71 96 13
Le Square des Photographes/6 Rue Saulnier, Puteaux, Fr . . . . (33)(45) 06 56 44
Lehtikuva Oy/Erottajankatu 9 B, Helsinki, Fin . . . . (358)(0) 64 85 00
Len Sirman Photos/27 Bout-du-Monde, Genf/GE, Switz . . . . (41)(22) 46 71 28
Les Ateliers Fol/2 Rue Cheneviere, Meylan, Fr . . . . (33)(76) 90 21 62
Life Press Agency/14 Rue Meslay, Paris, Fr . . . . (33)(1) 48 87 64 95
Lightmotif/27 Av du Devin-du-Village, Genf, Switz . . . . (41)(22) 45 97 00
Live Co Ltd/Kobayashichuo Bldg, Aoba-ku Sendai, Jp . . . .(81)(22) 224 1761
Lunte, Albert/Neumarkt 27, Zurich, Switz . . . . (41)(1) 251 92 74
Luxo/7 Fbg Annonciades, Annecy, Fr . . . . (33)(50) 51 91 27
Lynx/142 Rue Montmartre, Paris, Fr . . . . (33)(1) 42 36 62 56
Marco Polo/28 Rue Lauriston, Paris, Fr . . . . (33)(1) 47 04 21 19
Marie-Claire Copyright/11 bis Rue Boissy D'Anglas, Paris, Fr . . . . (33)(1) 42 66 87 38
Mariette, Catherine/Rue Etienenne Marcel, Montreuil, Fr . . . . (33)(1) 42 87 25 52
Masson, Evelyne/14 Rue Jean Cottin, Paris, Fr . . . . (33)(1) 46 07 18 78
Modes et Travaux Phototheque/10 Rue de la Pepeiniere, Paris, Fr . . . . (33)(1) 45 22 78 05
Multimedia-Photoscene AG/Anwandstr 34, Zurich, Switz . . . . (41)(1) 242 49 79
National Foto Persbureau bv/Heinzestraat 7, Amsterdam, Neth . . . . (31)(20) 76 05 55
National History Photographic Agency/57 High St, Sussex, UK 0444-89 25 14
National Medical Slide Bank/Chelmsford, UK . . . . (44)(245) 283351

National Trust/36 Queen Anne's Gate, London, UK . . . . (44)(71) 222 9251
Nature Photo Archives/Nervanderinkatu 11, Helsinki, Fin . . . . (358)(0) 409 238
Norsk Presse Service/Sorkedalsveien 10A, Oslo, Norw . . . . (47)(2) 69 44 95
NPS Stockholm AB/Box 11194, Stockholm, Swed . . . . (46)(8) 252 42 72
Odyssey Images/16 Rue du Fbg, Montmartre, Fr . . . . (33)(1) 45 23 21 37
Okapia Bildarchiv/Roderbergweg 168, Frankfurt, Switz . . . . (49)(69) 44 90 41
Olympia/Via Porpora 109-20131, Milan, Ital . . . . (39)(2) 26 14 22 22
Omnipress Int'l Photo Agency/Gevers Deynootweg 970k, Gravenhage, Neth . . . (31)(70) 354 67 67
Option Photo/6 Rue Paul Sezanne, Neuilly, Fr . . . . (33)(49) 44 30 00
Oxford Scientific Films Ltd/Lower Rd, Oxford, UK . . . . (44)(993) 881881
Pacific Press Service/Central Post Office 2051, Tokyo, Jp . . . . (81)(3) 3264-3821
Perceval/18 Rue Tholoze, Paris, Fr . . . . (33)(1) 42 54 69 77
Pet, Paul C/Herengracht 46d, Amsterdam, Neth . . . . (31)(20) 25 80 32
Petit Format/8 Rue D'Italie, Paris, Fr . . . . (33)(1) 45 88 98 66
Petit, Marie-Christine/39 Rue de L'Arbalete, Paris, Fr . . . . (33)(1) 43 36 24 65
Photo Bank Co/Nan-King E Rd, Taipei Taiwan, Jp . . . . (886)(2) 506 3220
Photographer's Library/81a Endell St, London, UK . . . . (44)(71) 836 5591
Phototheque Nationale/2 Ave Pasteur, Saint-Mande, Fr . . . . (33)(43) 28 68 59
Pictor International/Twyman House, London, UK . . . . (44)(1) 482 0478
Picture Box BV/Kruislaan 182, Amsterdam, Neth . . . . (31)(20) 668 10 51
Pitch/34 Rue Saint Dominique, Paris, Fr . . . . (33)(1) 45 51 62 80
Pix/106 Bd Arago, Paris, Fr . . . . (33)(1) 40 51 06 00
Planet Earth Pictures/4 Harcourt St, London, UK . . . . (44)(71) 262 4427
pm-Bild, Dr Peter Meyer/Scheibenstr 29, Bern/BE, Switz . . . . (41)(31) 41 32 41
Point of View/Hamburg/(49)(40) 222444 . . . . **pages 128-129**
Popper, Paul Ltd/Northampton/(44)(604) 414144 . . . . **page 179**
Potin, Annabelle/24 Rue Chabrol, Paris, Fr . . . . (33)(1) 42 46 68 65
Presser, Sem/Vondelstraat 96, Amsterdam, Neth . . . . (31)(20) 16 97 36
Prisma, Dia-Agentur + Bildprod uktion/Minervastr 33, Zurich, Switz . . . . (41)(1) 252 42 72
Publishing Affairs/Maja van Hoorn, Amsterdam, Neth . . . . (31)(20) 44 63 24 46
Punktum Bildarchiv/Klusstr 50, Zurich, Switz . . . . (41)(1) 55 45 40
Rapho/Rue D'Alger, Paris, Fr . . . . (33)(1) 42 60 30 06
Redfern, David/7 Bramley Rd, London, UK . . . . (44)(71) 792 9914
Reportagebild/Stockholm, Swed . . . . (46)(8) 788 05 00
Retrograph Archive Collection/164 Kensington Park Rd, London, UK . . . . (44)(71) 727 9378
Riel, Paul van/Voetboogstraat 26, Amsterdam, Neth . . . . (31)(20) 23 99 65
Rotulo, Catherine/11 Rue de Monttessuy, Paris, Fr . . . . (33)(1) 45 51 80 52
Sapporo Photo Live/5F Ishigaki Bldg, Chuoku Sapporo, Jp . . . . (81)(11) 222 1779
Schlapfer-Color/Abendweg 44, Luzern/LU, Switz . . . . (41)(41) 36 15 60
Schmidt, Albert/Felenstr 4, Sissach/BL, Switz . . . . (41)(61) 98 75 10
Science Photo Library/112 Westbourne Grv, London, UK . . . . (44)(71) 727 4712
Scope/Rue Eugene Millon, Paris, Fr . . . . (33)(1) 45 33 32 45
Scorpio/177 Rue D'Alesia, Paris, Fr . . . . (33)(1) 45 42 27 46
Scrito/23 Rue Bruyant, Reims, Fr . . . . (33)(26) 40 14 18
Sea and See/33 Rue Godot de Mauroy, Paris, Fr . . . . (33)(1) 42 65 16 60
Septier, Jean-Loup/5 Rue Antoine Vollon, Paris, Fr . . . . (33)(1) 46 28 11 03
SIE/Rome/(39)(6) 3241681 . . . . **page 144**
Sinus Fotoagentur/Kasinostr 19, Aarau/AG, Switz . . . . (41)(64) 22 24 72
Sipa Press/Paris/(33)(1) 47 43 47 43 . . . . **pages 6-7**
Six Jacques & Anne/36 Rue D'Hauteville, Paris, Fr . . . . (33)(01) 42 46 66 05
Sjoberg Press Service/Stockholm/(46)(8) 999 263 . . . . **pages 144,165-173**
Sonderegger, Christof/Haupstr 18, Rheineck/SG, Switz . . . . (41)(71) 44 40 88
South American Pictures/48 Station Rd, Woodbridge, UK . . . . (44)(394) 33963
Souverbie, Marie-Therese/8 Rue de la Folie Mericourt, Paris, Fr . . . . (33)(1) 48 05 84 87
Space Frontiers Ltd/30 Fifth Ave, Hampshire, UK . . . . (44)(705) 475313
Spectrum Reference Holland/Utrecht, Neth . . . . (31)(30) 406 37 37
Sport-Vision/5 Av de Lowendal, Paris, Fr . . . . (33)(1) 47 53 88 70
Sporting Pictures Ltd/7a Lambs Conduit Passage, London, UK . . . . (44)(71) 405 4500
Stam, Nico van der/2e Jacob van Campenstraat 96, Amsterdam, Neth . . . . (31)(20) 79 17 92
Stauss, Niklaus, Presse-Foto- Dienst/Predigerplatz 30, Zurich, Switz . . . . (41)(1) 251 08 08
Stills/5 Rue Laugier, Paris, Fr . . . . (33)(1) 47 63 82 40
Stock House/Hong Kong/(852)(5) 866-0887 . . . . **page 144**
Stock Image/22 Rue Villehardouin, Paris, Fr . . . . (33)(1) 48 04 00 09
Stock Photos/Castello 124-2 do C, Madrid, Sp . . . . (34)(1)564 4095
Stock Photos/Melbourne/(61)(3) 699-7600 . . . . **page 144**
Stock Photos/Sydney/(61)(2) 954-3988 . . . . **page 144**

This section of Black Book Stock encourages users of the book to work with some of the industry's leading suppliers. Each company provides an incentive offer on a series of coupons. While the incentives differ, all provide access to stock libraries that are among the most extensive available today.

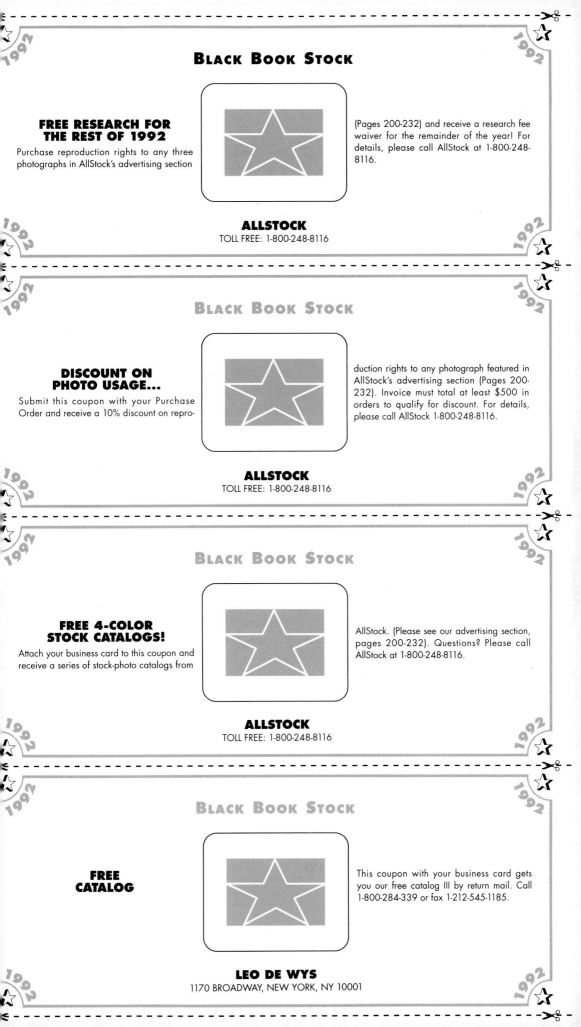

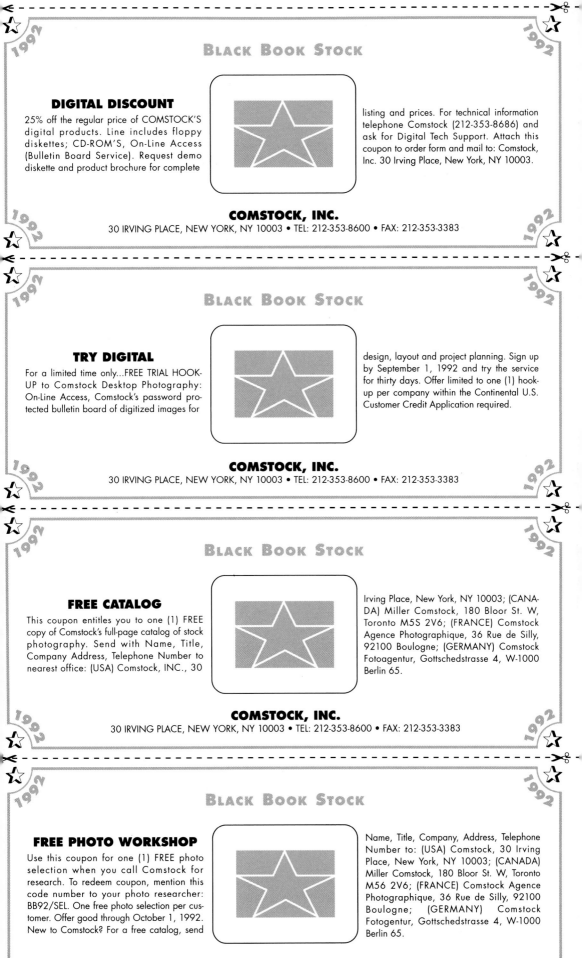

BLACK BOOK STOCK

Black Book Stock assumes no liability for fulfillment of this promotional offer, which is the sole responsibility of the advertiser.

BLACK BOOK STOCK

Black Book Stock assumes no liability for fulfillment of this promotional offer, which is the sole responsibility of the advertiser.

BLACK BOOK STOCK

Black Book Stock assumes no liability for fulfillment of this promotional offer, which is the sole responsibility of the advertiser.

BLACK BOOK STOCK

Black Book Stock assumes no liability for fulfillment of this promotional offer, which is the sole responsibility of the advertiser.

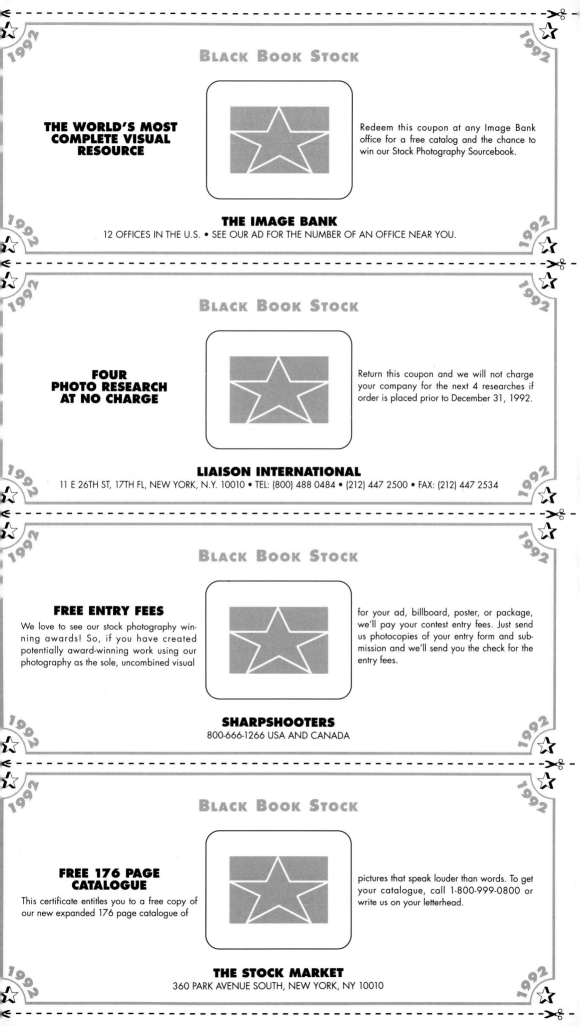

BLACK BOOK STOCK

Black Book Stock assumes no liability for fulfillment of this promotional offer, which is the sole responsibility of the advertiser.

BLACK BOOK STOCK

Black Book Stock assumes no liability for fulfillment of this promotional offer, which is the sole responsibility of the advertiser.

BLACK BOOK STOCK

Black Book Stock assumes no liability for fulfillment of this promotional offer, which is the sole responsibility of the advertiser.

BLACK BOOK STOCK

Black Book Stock assumes no liability for fulfillment of this promotional offer, which is the sole responsibility of the advertiser.

BLACK BOOK STOCK

Black Book Stock assumes no liability for fulfillment of this promotional offer, which is the sole responsibility of the advertiser.